NUMB

NUMB

Find Healing In Feeling

Kay Gackle, LMFT

ELM HILL

A Division of
HarperCollins Christian Publishing

www.elmhillbooks.com

Numb

Published in Nashville, Tennessee, by Elm Hill, an imprint of Thomas Nelson. Elm Hill and Thomas Nelson are registered trademarks of HarperCollins Christian Publishing, Inc.

Elm Hill titles may be purchased in bulk for educational, business, fund-raising, or sales promotional use. For information, please e-mail SpecialMarkets@ ThomasNelson.com.

All Scripture quotations, unless otherwise indicated, are taken from the Holy Bible, New International Version*, NIV*. Copyright © 1973, 1978, 1984, 2011 by Biblica, Inc.* Used by permission of Zondervan. All rights reserved worldwide. www.Zondervan.com. The "NIV" and "New International Version" are trademarks registered in the United States Patent and Trademark Office by Biblica, Inc.*

Library of Congress Cataloging-in-Publication Data

Library Congress Control Number: 2018960149

ISBN 978-1-400326372 (Paperback)
ISBN 978-1-400305926 (eBook)

CONTENTS

INTRODUCTION

As a therapist, I have seen so many clients unable to live a full life because they are numb. We reach a point where being numb becomes the new normal. This is either because we feel too much at once and shut down, or we make choices to shut down over time. Numb becomes our survival mode. In that mode, we don't maintain healthy relationships. Not with our spouses, our children, our friends, our coworkers, and most importantly with God. Survival mode is just that—doing the bare minimum to survive. I want this book to help you move from survival mode to healthy mode; to move from feeling numb to identifying and owning your feelings; to move from not being able to love anyone well to loving God, ourselves, and others well.

The Story

Katherine has been numb. For her, all the hard events of life had compounded. Right before her son's second birthday she suffered her first miscarriage, marking the beginning of a series of tough events for her and her husband. She bounced back from this miscarriage because they are common, and she had faith she would get pregnant again. That summer her grand-father, her papa, was diagnosed with a brain tumor and began what little treatment the doctors were able to offer him.

Shortly after his diagnosis, she found out she was pregnant again. This time was even more special because she would be sharing the experience with her sister who was expecting her first child. Around the same time, Katherine's grandmother, who suffered from Parkinson's disease, fell and was hospitalized. Katherine was nearing the end of her first trimester and went to her thirteen-week appointment for an ultrasound. Anxious to hear and to see the baby's heartbeat again, she instead heard the doctor say, "I am so sorry, Katherine." Katherine required surgery to remove the baby as soon as possible.

About a month later, her grandfather passed away. A few weeks after that, on December 23, her hometown church where she grew up, was baptized, and married, burnt down.

During all of these, medical bills were mounting. Standing in Target with no money to buy her son diapers, she cried. The new year began with her husband's grandfather's death, and in March she was forced to find a new job.

She and her husband continued to try to have another child, and although they explored different options, nothing was working. In August of that year, her husband's identical twin brother discovered he was in stage 4 of kidney failure and needed a transplant. Katherine buried her struggles while her husband underwent surgery to donate his kidney to his twin.

In January, her grandmother passed away. In September, she was hit by a drunk driver, totaling their only car. Being numb started to become her new normal.

A few months later, she learned that her sister-in-law was pregnant, which was bittersweet news in the midst of so much personal loss. Katherine found hope, however, when she too was pregnant soon after. A couple of weeks later, while her husband was across the country with his very ill stepfather, Katherine went in for an ultrasound. The baby, though thriving and growing, was in the fallopian tube, not the uterus. It was an ectopic pregnancy. Katherine required emergency surgery because it would be too dangerous and possibly fatal to delay. Her husband flew home on the red-eye that night, and on the next day, her son's fifth birthday, she had surgery to remove the baby and her right fallopian tube.

A week later her husband's stepfather died, and they went to California to celebrate his life and grieve the loss. A few months later, she was pregnant again but suffered her fourth miscarriage.

The feeling of defeat was setting in and her faith was being challenged. She had moments when she would sit in her closet and cry. She didn't smile for days. No one would blame Katherine for constantly being in survival mode; she was experiencing one blow after another. She began to experience anxiety and had her first short, but terrible, panic attack. Thankfully, Katherine had people in her life who encouraged her to seek professional help. She went through counseling, and the therapist was able to help her decrease the anxiety and work through the trauma of all she had experienced over the past few years.

The following year, she got pregnant again. Three weeks after telling family and friends the news, Katherine's mom was diagnosed with two primary, unrelated forms of cancer. That fall, her mom had surgery for both cancers one week apart. The breast cancer went into remission, and the colon cancer seemed at bay after radiation and chemotherapy treatments. Around this same time, Katherine and her husband found they had been inexplicably cut off from close family members. Though they desired and sought reconciliation, they were met with continual rejection. This was a different kind of loss from the one they had experienced before, but no less painful and without resolution.

A few months later her mom's colon cancer metastasized, and she continued treatments to slow it down but there would be no cure. Katherine's husband got a job that moved them from Florida to Oklahoma. Leaving behind family and friends who had journeyed with them through so many difficult times was yet another loss. As Katherine's mom's health steadily declined, Katherine moved back to her Florida hometown to care of her mom for the month prior to her passing. While this time was beneficial for both, it was incredibly difficult. Katherine added grieving the death of her mother to an already long list of losses. Though she had many feelings of pain and anxiety throughout these years, Katherine found herself numb.

While Katherine's story is unique, the feelings of loss that led to being numb are not. I don't just write this as a therapist, but as someone who has experienced these things ... all of them. Because Kay is short for Katherine, and this is my story.

This book is yours. Read it in a way that helps you most. Here is some helpful information moving forward as you dive into the book.

The Three Areas of Therapy

I had the privilege of working in a counseling center where the vision was to provide professional and clinical services in a Christian and holistic way. The entire counseling staff were Christians, but we offered services to anyone and tried to meet the needs to all who came to our offices. For the people who desired a Christian approach, I would often say that I believe there are three areas to explore when trying to find healing. These three areas are mental health disorders, trauma, and spiritual afflictions.

Exploring the first area consists of identifying whether there is a mental health disorder present. A diagnosable mental health disorder is one listed in the *Diagnostic and Statistical Manual of Mental Disorders* (DSM) and often we see symptoms that we can attribute to a certain diagnosis.

The second area is trauma. This is discovering whether trauma that has interrupted daily life functioning is present. Trauma is talked about more in Chapter 2, but it could be any adverse life event that has caused disruption or suffering.

The third area is spiritual affliction. In this area, we are answering the questions about whether there are current beliefs not grounded in truth, or if there are areas that need freedom.

For instance, a client comes in with anxiety. Anxiety could result from a mental health disorder, such as generalized anxiety disorder. It could be from trauma; a negative life event occurred and now there are triggers present that lead to anxiety. Lastly, it could be spiritual; living in fear, pain or shame, or having the need to forgive. It could also result from a combination of these three areas. The idea is that these three areas are not mutually exclusive of each other. Exploring each area in its entirety can give an individual a better picture of how to help find healing.

In this book, we focus on being numb in two of the three areas: trauma and spiritual affliction. Do we have trauma that has led us to where we are? Has life just beaten us up so much that we merely exist in it? The Bible recognizes, in Matthew, that our hearts can grow cold. Have we shut down our feelings so much that our hearts can't feel? Does abundant life feel like it's not an option? Maybe we don't feel the Holy Spirit or we feel like God is distant, and loving God, ourselves, and others well isn't possible right now.

If you suspect or know you have a diagnosable disorder, like posttraumatic stress disorder (PTSD) or clinical depression, I encourage you to seek professional counseling. Chapter 2's Self Care section contains additional information as well.

In the chapter, Spiritual Impact, the content has been taken from messages given by my husband, Greg, who is a pastor. His life passion is to help people find freedom by believing and genuinely knowing they are set free as an adopted child of God. He has assisted many in regard to forgiving themselves and others. His mentor in this area, Rob Porras, taught him about how we find ourselves living in fear, pain and shame. Greg has taken that and helped people shift their paradigms from fear to faith, pain to hope, and shame to love.

Self-Care

Throughout the book, you may find that we are discovering some deeper hurts that need more attention. You may realize there is trauma in a place where you hadn't really considered that previously. You may be triggered by a thought, feeling, or memory at some point while you are reading. This is completely normal. You may anticipate this by the title of some sections, but other sections may catch you off guard. In either case, be aware that self-care is needed. When you are simply going for a leisurely walk, you know you don't need to pack water, eat a certain meal, or rest up; on the other hand, when you are planning to do more rigorous exercise, you rest up, eat certain foods, and pack water. You plan for what you are about to encounter. In the same way, give attention to yourself if you are doing hard work throughout this book. If you need to seek a professional counselor or talk to a trusted person in your life, do that. If you need to take a little break, or sit with a section a little longer, do that. Whatever your self-care of rest, water, and food looks like for this journey, be aware of that and give it to yourself.

Engage

You may find it helpful to read the book first without answering all the questions in the Engage sections. I have found that some people like to answer as they go along, more like a workbook, while some like to read the content first and then go back and take the time to answer the questions. There is not a right or wrong way to read this book. It would be helpful to have a place to write notes and answers to the questions on which you have spent time reflecting. I hope this book will not only get you through this time of being numb, but that you will continue to use it as a tool or reference point in the future. You can date your notes and use them as a way to see where you have been before and how far you have come on whatever it is you are choosing to work. My desire for you is that the note pages will serve as an intentional place to answer the questions that come up in the book and as also an encouragement to you in the future.

CHAPTER 1

NUMB IS...

December 2007, Kay

*I woke up suddenly, and something seemed off. It was 5:00 a.m. on December 23rd. We were at my parents' house for the holidays, but at this moment, they weren't in their room. I tried to turn on the lights, and nothing was working. I called my mom worried that something was wrong. "The church burnt down a few hours ago," she said plainly. As I drove up to the church where I grew up, was baptized, married, and where my family still attended, I saw the black burnt pieces still smoking. I had no feeling. I wasn't sad and I wasn't mad; in fact, I tried to feel sad. I tried to feel. But I had nothing. I had two miscarriages within months, surgery, my grandfather's brain tumor, and death, financial burdens too heavy to fix, and now this. As I watched it continue to smolder, **I felt nothing as others cried around me.***

Numb simply means being unable to feel. It can be used to describe physical or emotional feelings. What's strange is the fact that medically, physical numbness is usually on the same list of symptoms as ache or pain. How can we feel both pain and be unable to feel simultaneously? Both can occur because even though we may experience feeling numb, the pain isn't gone. Medically, we feel physical numbness to an area of our body when our blood supply is cut off or diminished to that particular area, and our nerves don't send proper signals to our brain. The blood supply being cut off doesn't happen right away; instead, it can take a little bit of time. In a mild case, like our hand "falling asleep" at night, it usually happens in an hour or so. The blood flow is cut off because of a sleeping position and our brain can't receive the proper signals, so you get that tingling sensation of numbness. Frostbite is exposure to extreme cold. Our vessels can't sustain what it takes to get blood to our extremities, so it gets cut off. Our bodies jump into ultimate survival mode of trying to keep us going, no matter the cost.

Being emotionally numb can look similar. Becoming numb can happen over a bit of time as negative life events compound and pile on top of us. We react by addressing it as best as we can, but because we've had little recovery time, we stop feeling because all of these life events become too much to process. We head into survival mode, shut down, and go numb. The other way we go numb is from exposure to extreme trauma. We get hit with a major traumatic event, and it's too much to process at one time and we go into a survival mode. When in survival mode, we are getting up every morning even if it's a struggle; we are going to work; we are making sure ourselves and whomever we are responsible for is getting fed, dressed and where they need to be; we are paying bills; we are spending our time making sure everyday functioning is happening. We are "keeping our heads above water" and the "lights on in the house" per the clichés. At this point, relationships are suffering as well. Because relationships take work, it is an either-or scenario: *either* we are in survival mode *or* we are working on having healthy relationships. If we are numb, we are in survival mode. The blood supply is cut off and we are shut down. We can't feel anymore; there's nothing left. Then we get to a dangerous place where numb is our new normal. It starts to feel good not to feel. We think, *It's fine. At least I'm not consumed anymore or at least I am not upset. I am doing what I need to do. I am fine.*

The problem with not feeling the hard emotions (anger, sadness), is that we also are unable to feel the good emotions (joy, excitement). Our spectrum of feeling becomes significantly smaller. The feelings of deep sadness might be gone, but so are the feelings of deep joy. We are only able to experience within the small box below.

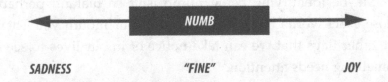

Where do we fall on the spectrum right now? Maybe we are numb right now and find ourselves in the box, or we recognize a time in our life where we once were numb. Whether it is recognizing you have been there in the past or are currently there, identifying what it looks like in our lives can help us move forward and be a starting point to find healing. My hope with this book is that we ask the tough questions, give the freedom to explore this topic, and be the healthiest version of ourselves.

A phrase that we might say when we are numb is, "I just didn't feel—I was numb." I have heard those exact words said so many times by others and myself. We feel an emptiness inside, and we describe it as numb. Or maybe we feel like our brain is in a bit of fog; we hear conversations around us or we see people around us, but it is as if nothing penetrates. Others' stories about life, either good or bad, don't seem to affect us at all. We are just kind of existing. We are "fine." If we aren't currently there, it might take some time to go back and think through some life events or moments when it was difficult, but be encouraged to do the work and spend time thinking about this. Identifying a time or circumstance when we have felt numb will be our focus throughout the book. It will offer a real life, concrete example instead of abstractly thinking through this concept. Also, as we do our own work, we can then help others that might identify themselves as numb.

Maybe identifying being numb isn't so blatant; perhaps those exact words haven't come out of our mouth yet. There are other flags that we can take notice of in our lives to see if something needs attention.

Underreaction

One flag can be a lack or muting of your feelings. It sounds obvious, but most of us do not pay attention to our feelings. We

4

talk more about feelings later in the book, but for now, think about how you express joy, excitement, happiness, gratitude, anger, sadness, and hurt. Maybe it has been a while since you felt them or the intensity of your emotions is different from those around you, like in the opening story of this chapter. Underreaction can show you that you are only feeling "fine," or within the blue box. Nothing is too sad or too joyful.

Overreaction

Another flag can be your emotions or reactions not matching a given situation. Maybe we find ourselves overly crying when watching a commercial. Or there is yelling and acting with rage at a person when they cut us off on the road. While these things are sure to elicit some emotion or reaction, is the intensity of the feeling or behavior in which they are happening appropriate for what's going on at the moment? An intense response of emotion that comes as a shock, either to ourselves or others, is worthy of notice. This type of reaction can be a flag that there is some work to do. Sometimes we can hit a nerve in the midst of being numb, and a pain signal goes off surprisingly. Asking why and digging a little more in-depth can help to figure out what is off within us. Feelings will be discussed later in chapter four.

Distractions

A third flag to consider is if we have current distractions that keep us from feeling. We can distract ourselves intentionally or unintentionally and in ways that are either healthy or unhealthy. For example, exercising to keep ourselves from thinking, or eating food to offer ourselves comfort; using alcohol or drugs to medicate the pain, or hurting ourselves as a way to feel. We will go more into how we sometimes self-medicate, but for now, just confirm if that's happening. If it is, note it as a flag and try to determine the situation or the feelings that are being avoided. It will serve us as we read the next chapters.

Relationally

Feeling disengaged, withdrawn, or not invested in relationships can be a flag. One of the hardest parts of life is engaging in relationships when we are numb or having trouble feeling. We may be present physically, but our minds and hearts are elsewhere. In normal circumstances, we call friends to say hello, or we show empathy when someone we know is going through a difficult time. However, when we are numb, those tasks seem difficult. We may not have the energy to care for others because we can barely take care of ourselves.

Spiritually

If your relationship with God has changed, that can also be a flag. If the Bible doesn't penetrate into our life when we read it, or if we have trouble identifying the Holy Spirit's work and presence in our life, we may be spiritually numb. We may still believe in our faith, but there is not much else going on in our spiritual relationship. We feel shut down.

Being numb spiritually or emotionally can also affect the other parts of our life. It's important to take time to see what flags are present; there may be more than one flag present in more than one area.

As a therapist, I've seen clients who, when asked about a situation or area in their life, say they are "over" it, meaning it doesn't bother them anymore. Later we discover that in reality, he or she (or they as a couple) has not done the work needed, and numbness has taken over, often for good reason. The clients have exhausted the conversation about it, they are tired of the pain, they see the pain coming and detach themselves pre-emptively, or they just cannot think about it anymore. It could be that the situation hasn't changed, and they are in what feels like an endless cycle. It may feel to them like they are "over" it, but in truth it has become a silent landmine. We begin to think that numbness is a healthy way to live, and we convince ourselves we are being strong. It takes work to dig for answers and to make time in our hectic lives to sit and think about the answers to those questions. Most people don't give themselves vacations, let alone time to just sit and reflect on questions that can lead to not-so-fun feelings. I ask that as we read this book, we would give ourselves some time, truth, and grace as we start to explore where we are and heal from being numb.

It may feel to them like they are "over" it, but in truth it has become a silent landmine.

Starting now, if you decide to work as you go, you may use your note pages to answer the following questions:

Engage

- Am I currently numb? Or do I remember a time when I was numb? When I think about certain areas or situations in my life, which ones bring relief that I can't feel anything about them?
- When was the last time I felt extreme joy, excitement, happiness, or gratitude? In general? Or about the specific situation or area of life that has me numb?
- When was the last time I felt anger, sadness, or hurt? In general? Or about the specific situation or area of life that has me numb?
- In what areas do my emotions not appropriately match the given situation? When does my behavior or my reaction not match the situation?
- Am I distracting myself so that I don't feel?
- Do I love myself, God, and others well? How am I doing that?
- Are there other flags present in my life?

CHAPTER 2

How We Become Numb

April 2010, Kay

*I knew we had a lot going on in our lives, but I was grieving when I needed to and also taking time for myself when I needed it. I was processing as much as I could and had so many friends who were checking in on me, which is why the next event caught me off guard. I was sitting on a plane headed to Nicaragua with my son and my husband when my heart started racing. I felt like I couldn't breathe and all I wanted to do was get off the plane, but I was unable. I was stuck on there. I got up to get some cold water and the flight attendant told me I needed to sit down because we were taking off. I recognized it from hearing others' stories: I was having a panic attack. It eventually passed, thank goodness. **I thought I had processed all that was happening to me**; I was so intentional about feeling when I needed to feel—why am I having anxiety now? It didn't go away; it wasn't isolated, I had other incidents after that. I realized there was just too much to process and feel, and I was more numb than I thought.*

We can get numb from a flood of emotions at one time or a decision to not feel over time. Getting numb from a flood of emotions happens when we are in a situation that is traumatic, and much like the physical, the emotional heart shuts down so that we can survive. Physically, the body shuts down blood flow to extremities to keep the core warm; emotionally, we shut down because if we felt every emotion, we would not be able to function in everyday life. We simply could not get out of bed, brush our teeth, or eat, so instead, we become numb in order to operate. This is not bad. This is a protection mechanism inside us.

We can get numb from a flood of emotions at one time or a decision to not feel over time.

It is beneficial both physically and emotionally when our body shuts our heart down to help us survive by keeping us moving and functioning daily. Ideally, as time and healing happen, and as necessary functioning isn't our primary goal anymore, we can begin to feel again. We can process the grief and sift through the leftover flood of emotions. However, there can come a time when we are past the initial trauma, we have been functioning for a while, and still find ourselves unable to feel. We find ourselves numb. It is at this moment when the questions and reflections can be helpful to move us to a new place of healing.

Other times we prolong a decision to not feel. We may start to feel, and then tell ourselves phrases like:

"Not now, I am working, I'll have to deal with this later."

"Not now, not in front of the kids, I have to be strong."

"Not now, I don't want to spend any more time crying about this or being angry about this."

"This is not worth it, I'm fine."

Most of those statements are not inherently wrong. The problem begins when we don't deal with it later, or we are always strong for the kids and we never take time for ourselves to sift through what's going on inside of us. As we think about our day, when do we reflect intentionally? Do we have a regular time whether it's daily, weekly, monthly, or even yearly when we allow ourselves to reflect on our life? Most people get up in the mornings, have some breakfast, go to work or school, do some sort of activity, eat some dinner, finally sit down after the long day, maybe watch some TV, then go to bed. Get up, repeat. Truthfully, we don't have time in our lives the way the world is now. In the car, we turn on music, listen to an audio book, or talk on the phone. Rarely do we use that time to think about what has been happening in our lives. If we don't get to this regularly, we will miss out on healing. Likewise, if we only give ourselves this time once a year, there is much that we would need to reflect on that we would forget. Doing this daily allows for a quick check-in of all that happens in a day. If we can't get to it that day, then we need to make note so that we can efficiently come back to it. There are days when the check-in will go fast because it was a decent day. Then there are days, and events that happen in a day, that require a little more time processing. The idea is that we don't prolong the decision to feel what we need to feel. We make note of it and we don't shut ourselves down. Acknowledging the feeling or feelings, in itself, brings healing.

Trauma

Trauma is an interesting word. I imagine very few of us would label our own life events as trauma. However, if we were to rate whether someone else's story would be considered a trauma, most likely we would say yes. People tend to minimize the trauma of their own stories. Imagine someone sharing your story as their own. If we heard that story, would we think it was traumatic? There are many definitions of trauma. The American Psychological Association defines trauma "as an emotional response to a terrible event like an accident, rape or natural disaster." (apa.org) *Webster Dictionary* defines it as "a disordered psychic or behavioral state resulting from severe mental or emotional stress or physical injury." (Merriam-Webster.com).

Trauma causes an emotional response, a disruption or suffering in one's life.

Some trauma experts divide trauma into big T traumas and little t traumas. Big T traumas would include catastrophic events, while little t traumas would be less on the catastrophic scale yet still cause an emotional response or suffering. In this book, trauma is less defined by the event and more by the response resulting from the event. Trauma causes an emotional response, a disruption or suffering in one's life. Now looking at our own life, would we say that we have experienced some type of trauma, either big T or little t? Would we consider divorce in that category? Even though multiple people have suffered due to divorce, does that mean that it is no longer a trauma? At times I have heard people say, "Well, lots of people deal with *this* (whatever their "this" is) in their lives, so I don't think it's a trauma." If I ask us to describe what happened as a result of an event and how it has affected our life since, we have experienced a trauma if we had a strong emotional response that disrupted our lives and caused suffering. I don't say this to make us all victims of life and trauma. I say this so we don't minimize what we already feel and we don't assume we "should or shouldn't" be feeling a certain way about it. We can get stuck in life when we force ourselves not to feel a certain way, and I am encouraging us all to give ourselves the freedom to feel. It is there so that we can make a decision what to do with those feelings in our life, otherwise they can end up managing us and we won't even thoroughly know it. We need to ask ourselves the hard questions and see what happens there. We can't assume, based on others' experiences, that we have not had trauma or that we should or shouldn't feel a certain way. Trauma is the response resulting from an event that causes disruption or suffering, and not giving time for reflection can lead us to become numb.

Sometimes in trauma, an event happens that results in the need for us to forgive. Whether it is ourselves or others who need the forgiveness, recognizing this will help in discovering if we are numb. Often, unforgiveness is another reason for becoming numb. Unforgiveness keeps you in bondage to the pain, and always holding on the hurt, the offense, and/or the offender. In essence, we are re-traumatizing ourselves over and over. We will discuss forgiveness in depth in chapter 8.

Engage

- What led me to be numb?
- What traumas have I experienced?
- Was it a single event trauma, or were there multiple events?
- What is/was my response to those traumas?
- How has the event or events affected my life since they happened? What disruptions or suffering did it cause in my life?
- Have I been pushing aside my feelings, and (or) is there more processing I need to do in regards to my trauma?
- Do I need to forgive someone within my trauma?

Whether it is a recurring choice to "come back to it later" or a flood of emotions that happened at once causing a shut down as a coping mechanism, the result can be the same. Our hearts become numb and because of that, we find ourselves merely existing. As we journey, we need to be willing to go where our mind takes us and notice what is happening within us while we are doing that; when we do, we will begin to learn what has led us to where we are now.

Self-care

If you have experienced a trauma and have not sought professional counseling, please consider whether it would be helpful. This book is not a substitute for professional counseling.

If you are reexperiencing the event through flashbacks, night-mares, thoughts or memories, or physical/emotional triggers; if you are avoiding people or memories connected to the event; feeling stuck in severe emotions, isolated or detached, memory problems related to the event, or negative changes in mood; difficulty concentrating, irritability, difficulty falling asleep or staying asleep, hypervigilance—then these are some flags to indicate needed professional help with your trauma.

Also, if you have experienced depression with symptoms including depressed mood for most the day, nearly every day; markedly diminished interest or pleasure in all, or almost all, activities most of the day; weight loss or weight gain; not able to sleep or wanting to sleep all the time; feelings of restlessness or being slowed down; loss of energy nearly every day; feelings of worthlessness or guilt; diminished ability to concentrate or make decisions; recurrent thoughts of death or suicide, or plan for committing suicide—please seek professional help. (DSM V)

CHAPTER 3

PROBLEMS AND SYMPTOMS OF BEING NUMB

April 2016, Steven

I know I am numb. So much has been going on with the recent divorce and sorting out what new life even looks like to me. The fights over who gets what, the loss of what life was supposed to look like, the hurtful words coming out of the person who had said they loved me not too long ago, the kids and their faces as they try and figure out what is happening, the need and desire to protect them from the hurt and confusion—it's all too much. **I am so relieved not to be crying or angry or hurt anymore.** *I know numb probably isn't a good thing, but I am in no hurry to feel all of that again.*

For some of us, we might be happy that we aren't feeling at the moment. It might feel like a relief. Take that time of relief. Also, remember staying there too long can make it harder to feel again. What we end up doing is using emotional and physical energy to do triage on ourselves instead of dealing with the hurt. There are some actual problems with being numb. Some of us know it's a problem being numb and some of us need to see what the issues are and then figure out if we are just treating those issues instead of finding healing.

Problem: We only feel "fine," and we miss out on feeling deep joy.

Symptom: We say "I'm fine," don't experience feeling really high or really low.

The statement "I'm fine" is often heard when someone is asked, "How are you doing?" It's the easy, quick answer to what could be a very loaded question. Coming up with "Fine," regarding the spectrum, places us in the middle. We don't necessarily feel bad all the time, but we don't feel joy or happiness. We have a horrible day at work and we might feel bad but it doesn't go so deep that it really affects us. We have a really great day at work, and we might feel good, but it doesn't penetrate and doesn't last. Someone asks us about a loss we just went through (recently a relationship fell apart, lost a job, kids are really struggling, parents are declining in health, not doing well in school, aren't performing well, finances are really tight) and we don't really feel anything about it, and so we answer with "Fine." We are numb. We can't be fully engaged in whatever is really happening when we are numb. There is a big difference between saying, "Despite all of ____, I am doing okay," and saying, that we are "fine." The first is present and engaged in the feeling of what is going on, the latter is half-engaged and unable to be present at all in the situation. We don't feel the bad as deep but, on the flip side, we never get to feel and appreciate the good as deeply either. Some people have come to think of this as a skill, the "I don't let things get to me" skill.

While there is emotional intelligence in how we react to emotions, there is no intelligence in not feeling them at all.

While there is emotional intelligence in how we react to emotions, there is no intelligence in not feeling them at all. The skill and intelligence comes with recognizing your emotions, regulating your emotions, and reacting appropriately to your emotions. Saying we are fine because we don't feel so bad or feel so good (being in the middle of the spectrum) is a red flag. Red flags mean it is time to do some further inspection and reflection to see if we are really not fine after all.

Engage

- Is this problem or symptom present in my life currently or has it been at one time?
- How and where do I see the symptoms showing up? What is the context of them in my life?

Problem: We minimize our feelings, and we can't fully heal.

Symptom: We only think about the situation for short amount of time, we brush it off when asked about it, or we just wait for it to get better on its own.

We minimize the actual situation, thus minimizing our feelings. We give ourselves 15 minutes thinking that should be enough time, and then we tell ourselves that this situation or area of life is "not that big of a deal." Often clients come in and tell me they can't figure out why they can't "fix" themselves. When the story is said back to them as if it were the therapist's story with the question, "If this was my story, what would you say?" the client is shocked at how difficult, sad, and even traumatic their story is when someone else says it.

I find that most people are too tough on themselves. They can show empathy for others and even hear other people's stories yet, when it comes to their own, they minimize it. They think it should not be this big of a deal, that they should be "over it" already and that it's nothing compared to someone else's struggle. Having perspective of what we are going through is both wise and good. Likewise, realizing that we might need to spend more time on our own healing shows wisdom as well. As we minimize our story, we begin to shut down any feelings associated with it because it's not working, changing, or getting better.

Engage

- Is this problem or symptom present in my life currently or has it been at one time?
- How and where do I see the symptoms showing up? What is the context of them in my life?
- Write down your story with another name inserted instead of your name. Reread it as if it belonged to someone else.
- What would you tell that person? Is it worth spending some time figuring it out and working on it?

Problem: We distract ourselves to the point where we create an unhealthy synaptic connection in our brain.

Symptom: We choose to self-medicate with our drug of choice.

We medicate ourselves with drugs, food, pornography, exercise, alcohol, people. A distraction is anything that can replace the negative feeling and instead helps our brains focus on something else instead of the pain. We get into a cycle: we feel the pain, we don't think we can handle it or we don't want to think about it, and we attempt to avoid it through the distraction of choice. The more we self-medicate, the more we strengthen a new synapse in our brain. Because the wiring eventually changes, we even stop recognizing the triggers that cause us to feel. We no longer need to feel bad to self-medicate, we just medicate. So begin addictions, secrets, and lies to continue with the addiction.

Maybe we aren't addicted to drugs or one of those pre-viously listed, but we find ourselves looking to outside distractions to fill our time and make us feel better. We jump from activity to activity, or person to person to fulfill it. We busy ourselves with the "important" and convince ourselves we are "fine." The busyness can begin to create rewards in our brain, a high of dopamine when we choose over and over to distract ourselves this way. While ignoring the pain may lessen it temporarily, we create silent landmines that will blow up later when we don't address it. The best way to man-age trauma is to face it head on.

Self-Care

If you find yourself in addiction, please seek help from a professional counselor or professional program. Or if this feels overwhelming to face it, please seek out professional counsel-ing or a trusted a friend who can walk with you and get you the help needed. But don't cover it up; face it and find healing.

Engage

- Is this problem or symptom present in my life currently or has it been at one time?
- How and where do I see the symptoms showing up? What is the context of them in my life?
- Do you find yourself turning to one these distractions for comfort?

- Have they become so regular that you find yourself addicted or in need of only turning to that to feel better?

Problem: We pseudo-bandage the hurt, so it never really heals.

Symptom: We ignore the pain, hurt, or triggers.

When dealing with physical injuries, we protect them by putting on a bandage. We place the injury in a temporary holding pattern so some healing can happen. When this is done for too long, however, we actually prolong healing. In the same way, emotionally, we leave the bandage on by not wanting to face it or bring up the hurt. We believe if we don't touch it, it won't hurt. We say statements like, "It's just better to not go there right now," or we are "waiting for time to heal." In our waiting, we push the pain and hurt down to where we think it will disappear. We find ourselves ignoring triggers that we experience related to the hurt. We make ourselves so good at avoiding reality that we walk around with a bandage on while pretending it doesn't exist. The bandage may be needed temporarily, but eventually it will need to be taken off so full healing can happen. Not addressing the reality of what is happening in and around you does not mean that it will just go away. It will prolong healing and you will most likely add more injuries trying to "protect" this one.

Engage

- Is this problem or symptom present in my life currently or has it been at one time?
- How and where do I see the symptoms showing up? What is the context of them in my life?
- Is there a pain or hurt that you find yourself working really hard at protecting?
- Do you find yourself just waiting for the injury to 'just go away'? Are you waiting for time to pass so it won't be as painful?
- What triggers have you been ignoring related to the hurt?
- Are you expecting people or yourself to forget the pain and then move on like it didn't exist?

Problem: We have relationships that begin to suffer.

Symptom: We are in unhealthy relationships.

We cannot give what we do not have. We provide out of the overflow. Our relationship with God and our relationships with others both suffer. We start to spend so much energy and time on not feeling that we don't have much left over to love God, ourselves, or others. If we are numb and protecting our injury or self-medicating, we are in a destructive pattern of not feeling and not letting others into your life. We cannot have both trust and secrets or lies in deep, meaningful relationships. We were made to do life with others, and once we start to shut down the feelings, we begin to shut down relationships. That is why relationships start to suffer. Healthy relationships have these present: mutual respect, trust, honesty, excellent communication with listening and sharing, support, and equal give and take. If we are "fine," we will love in a "fine" way but nothing more. The profound joy that a relationship can provide and the joy we can offer in a relationship will not exist.

Relationships affect communities, cities, states, nations, world, businesses, families, churches, education—our everyday lives. All of these get affected when we choose to stay "fine" and not do the work to feel and be emotionally healthy. Relationships and emotional health need and influence each other, either positively or negatively. Negatively, the cycle spirals into the following: the more we ignore the work of processing and are emotionally unhealthy, the more unhealthy our relationships will be; and the more unhealthy our relationships are, the more we are emotional unhealthy. This cycle spirals downward into more emotional unhealthiness and suffering relationships. Conversely, emotional health and relationships can positively help each other. When we choose to do the work of being emotionally healthy, the better our relationships will be. In a research study in the *Journal of Health and Social Behavior*, Umberson and Montez found in regards to social relationships and health that "[S]social ties can instill a sense of responsibility and concern for others that then lead individuals to engage in behaviors that protect the health of others, as well as their own health." (J Health Soc Behav. Author manuscript; available in PMC 2011 Aug 4., https://www.ncbi.nlm.nih.gov/pmc/articles/PMC3150158/; D. Umberson and J.K. Montez)

When you choose to stay numb, you are affecting more than just yourself.

Engage

- Is this problem or symptom present in my life currently or has it been at one time?
- How and where do I see the symptoms showing up? What is the context of them in my life?
- Is it really possible to simultaneously not feel and yet still love well? What does that relationship look like?
- Do your relationships have the following present: mutual respect, trust, honesty, excellent communication with listening and sharing, support, and equal give and take? Are your relationships healthy?
- Would the people in your life say the same?

Being numb leads to problems not just in our own lives but also in the lives of others we love. It takes courage and time to sit down and ask ourselves these questions. It takes honesty to answer them truthfully. If we are willing to do the work, we can find healing.

CHAPTER 4

ALL THE FEELINGS

April 2010, Kay

*I was sitting in the hospital bed waiting for the anesthesia to wear off. I was listening to my doctor tell me that it was good we did the surgery because it could have been fatal. If I went one more day, or if the tube had burst, there would not have been time to save me. It was a successful surgery, but they had to removed my right fallopian tube. **I felt nothing**. I wasn't crying. I wasn't sad. I was numb. I listened to every word and though I can remember it all, I am not sure at that moment if it really sank in fully.*

Often it is heard, "I just feel numb." This is a bit of an ironic statement. Is it a feeling if we "feel" nothing? We understand the statement as thinking about a situation that appropriately would bother us, yet we feel nothing. Being numb can be considered a feeling the same as white is considered a color. In the color wheel, regarding pigment, the color white appears because it absorbs no color. White is literally the absence of color. In the same way, the numb feeling is the absence of feeling. The color white can be seen when it is against a background of other colors. Likewise, we recognize being numb against the knowledge of where other feelings would typically exist. We know that we would typically feel in a certain way, but we just don't feel anything. We share our stories of what has happened or is happening to us and see others reacting to our situation and we feel nothing. We see a movie, TV show, or commercial that alludes to our situation and feel nothing. Or we think about our situation and feel nothing. We might get bothered by it, but other than that it's white, it's blank, there's nothing there. We "feel" numb because we know there's more. There's more to feel and there's more to experience, yet it seems we can't get there. We recognize the numbness rather than feeling it. We realize that where we used to experience a feeling, there is now only emptiness. We try and make ourselves feel something, but nothing happens. We think about a situation and we come up blank. We are numb.

Feeling Feelings

A movie that frequently comes on during the holiday season is the recent version of *The Grinch Who Stole Christmas*. The

Grinch was rejected by the Whos, the group of people whom he grew up with, as a child and because of that hurt, he finally decides to shut down his heart. As Christmas approaches, the Grinch plots to steal all of Whoville's presents and stop the holiday. However, in a turn of events, the Grinch realizes Christmas is about something more than the items he can take away. He hears their singing and sees their love despite the gifts being gone. With this realization, the Grinch's heart begins to work again. As his heart begins to pump louder, he falls to the ground, grabs his heart, and painfully yells to his dog, "Help! I'm feeling!" This is my favorite part of the movie because of its accuracy. We may not fall to the ground when we begin to feel, but our feelings can be overwhelming and even painful at times. Maybe we aren't entirely sure what is happening to our bodies when we begin to feel again. Learning about feelings and what we can do with them can help us as we begin to move away from being numb.

Learning about feelings and what we can do with them can help us as we begin to move away from being numb.

One reason why people are so confused by this subject is that there is not a great definition of the word "feeling." It is, at best, obscure, and seems to mostly address the physical sense of the word, "the awareness of your body of something in it or on it." (http://www.merriam-webster.com/dictionary/feeling) There is another definition in the dictionary that says, "an emotional state or reaction." This definition leads us to the second reason that adds confusion. The words emotion and feeling are often used interchangeably. In our everyday vernacular, though, we tend to say, "I feel..." versus stating the emotion. The word "emotion" on the same dictionary website is defined as "a strong feeling (such as love, anger, joy, hate, or fear)." Neither word is defined without using the other one. This makes trying to decipher what each of them is a bit more difficult. Thirdly, feeling is not a simple process; it's complex. There are many theories and studies of what happens in the brain and when it occurs during the process of feeling or having emotions. This complexity adds to the difficulty in making a simple definition. For this book, to eliminate confusion moving forward, a definition and common understanding are needed. We will use the word "feeling," and not emotion, mostly because of how we talk about feelings in everyday language. "Feeling" will encompass a larger umbrella definition and "feelings" will speak more to the label and identifiers of feeling. The definition of the verb "feeling" will be the awareness of and experiencing what's happening around you or to you and being conscious of your inner state. The definition of the noun "feelings" will be the identified reaction to your feeling such as anger, sadness, happiness, etc.

> Our feelings are an indicator. They indicate to us that there is something we need to notice.

Feelings have gotten a bad rap because of some frequently quoted sentiments in our culture.

"You can't rely on your feelings."

"Don't be overemotional."

"The heart is deceitful above all things, and beyond cure. Who can understand it?" Jeremiah 17:9

The danger here is the tendency to discount our feelings when they arise. We tell ourselves to suppress what is going on inside of us because we can't trust it anyway. Suppressing feelings is an unproductive road to go down. Our feelings are an indicator. They indicate to us that there is something we need to notice. If we are angry, then why are we angry? If we are sad, then why are we sad? If we are happy, afraid, excited or surprised, then why are we feeling that way? If we are reacting to what is happening around us, whether appropriately or inappropriately matching the situation, this is still something worthy to notice. From here we can make choices, but awareness needs to come first. If we are unaware of what we are feeling and what is happening around us and to us, we cannot choose to do anything about it. This is when our feelings become in charge of our behavior. Instead, we need to slow the process down, hit the pause button, and learn what to do from there.

Sad. Mad. Glad.

The primary colors on a color wheel are red, blue, and yellow. Let's consider the primary feelings as sad, mad, and glad. Out of the three primary colors come secondary colors when we mix two of the primary colors—orange, purple, and green. Six more tertiary colors are created from this. Likewise, if we say the primary feelings are sad, mad, and glad, then mixing them in different combinations should give many other colors of feelings—disappointment, frustration, anxiety, fear, nervousness, shame, excitement, pleasure, elation, joy, etc. Sometimes getting to the root of a feeling is difficult. When you are trying to feel, are unable to feel, or have been pushing feelings aside for so long, it can seem foreign. It can help to break down and recognize the feeling we are experiencing. For example, take the color indigo. At first glance, it's easy to label it as that known color and move on from there. However, if we were to look a little closer and think about how indigo came to be a color, we see there's more to it. When unpacked, this known color is blue + purple, which is really blue + blue + red. In the same way, we label a known feeling like frustration and we move on instead of taking time to figure out why we are frustrated or how we got that way. We might put it off on a circumstance or a person who "made us" frustrated. Sometimes, there is really more underneath that can help us detect what is going on if we just sit with our feelings and dig a little deeper. For example, we start out as sad, and when we can't sustain feeling sadness any longer, it can shift to feeling angry. Then that mixture looks like frustration on smaller things because that is more manageable than dealing with the original sadness that seems overwhelming. Obviously, our feelings and emotions are more complex than sad, mad, or glad, but the idea is that the surface level of our emotions may have a few layers below it.

Feelings Guide

Digging into what we are feeling and what emotions we are having is always worth our time and energy. Asking why and looking for the how will help us be detectives and ultimately find more healing. Often we just simply say what we think we should feel based on context of our situation. This guide reverses that order and starts with noticing our feelings first. My friend and colleague, Vicki Gray, LCSW, and I created the guide to help people see the process on paper. It is a simple process to follow. We typically do all these steps pretty quickly and without a great deal of intentional thought. The challenge is to slow the process down in the moment and to put intentional thought into each of the four steps. Slowing down also exposes where we might have default actions based on specific feelings. Taking the time to think about and write down what we are experiencing helps us not to act on default, and instead choose with intentionality.

Feelings Guide

Feel it.

What are you physically feeling?

_____

Name it.

What is the name of the feeling you are experiencing?

_____

Truth it.

What facts or events triggered these feelings?
Do these feelings match the situation?
Are there any other influencers present?

_____
_____
_____

Choose it.

List all action options, positive and negative.
Choose which one you will live out.

_____
_____
_____
_____

Feel it.

Feel what is happening around and to you. Don't brush it off as if it doesn't exist. Don't dismiss this part by skipping it and moving straight to truth or telling yourself you shouldn't be feeling this way. Feelings are important because they are indicators. There is something to notice regardless of whether or not we decide to act on that feeling. Pause. Notice what is happening physically to you as you feel. Physically we experience sensations when we feel. Identify how you would describe the physical feelings of the way your body reacts to those. Some physical sensations for sadness include stomach hurting or a feeling like you were kicked in the stomach, feeling a lump in your throat, heart aches or feeling heavy, frowning eyebrows or mouth, or there are tears. Some physical sensations of anger might include your face getting red, hot or flushed, heart pounding, clenched fists, shoulders' muscles tighten, furrowed eyebrows or the urge to hit something. Physical sensations for gladness might induce smiling, urge to jump or move, or heart feels light. If you are grateful, your heart might feel full or cry tears of joy. If you are excited, your stomach might get butterflies or your heart might race slightly. Become a detective of your feelings by observing, gathering facts of what you are experiencing, and collecting evidence to show what you are feeling. Bring awareness to what you are experiencing by being fully present in the moment.

Name it.

Name the feeling or feelings that you are noticing. Dig deeper here and identify what feelings are at play. A research study completed by UCLA and supported by the National Institute of Health says that putting a feeling into words produces therapeutic effects in the brain.

"When people see a photograph of an angry or fearful face, they have increased activity in a region of the brain called the amygdala. This serves as an alarm to activate a cascade of biological systems to protect the body in times of danger. Scientists see a robust amygdala response even when they show such emotional photographs subliminally, so fast a person can't even see them. But does seeing an angry face and simply calling it an angry face change our brain response? The answer is yes according to Matthew D. Lieberman, UCLA associate professor of psychology and a founder of social cognitive neuroscience."

Lieberman also references popular psychology that says, "When you're feeling down, just pick yourself up, but the world doesn't work that way. If you know you're trying to pick yourself up, it usually doesn't work—self-deception is difficult. Because labeling your feelings doesn't require you to want to feel better, it doesn't have this problem." We can't just pick ourselves up or just get over something. It helps to name the feeling; that alone gives us therapeutic effects in our brain. Our feelings cause biological responses in our brains, which is why we cannot ignore them. Recognize there is power in identifying and naming a feeling. There are also little nuances to feelings, and naming it appropriately will help us to ultimately better choose what to do with it. Are you sad or despaired? Are you frustrated or angry? Are you discouraged or are you disappointed? Are you feeling rejected or lonely? Whatever the feeling, name it well.

Truth it.

Write down the truth, the facts, and the events about the situation that got you to this place. Analyze the truth and your reaction to it. Does the named feeling match the situation? Is this feeling reliable to act on or not? Are there current triggers from past experiences? Sometimes a past experience will create triggers for us. A trigger can be anything—hurtful words that were said in the past that get repeated or a past inuring action of some sort occurs in a current context. When triggers occur, it takes you back to the negative experience. You need to ask yourself if your feelings are a result of a trigger. Are there other parts of your story influencing your reaction? Perhaps it is more general than a specific trigger. A past way of life, learned culture, or the way you grew up could influence a current feeling, especially if it is rubbing up against a different way of life or culture. Are there multiple factors at play? You can react to a less significant situation in a more significant way when life seems to pile up. Are you overreacting or underreacting? Perhaps it is an appropriately named feeling but there is overreaction to it. Maybe you are underreacting and need to examine the named feeling to better identify what you are experiencing.

It might be helpful to think of a scale when trying to determine if we are overreacting or underreacting. In the hospital, a nurse will often ask you how much pain you are experiencing. They have their own measure to know if it's unbalanced. On day one postsurgery, they might expect a 6 or 7. As the days progress, the expected number goes down in relation to the pain. In the same way, we can establish a ratings scale of 1 to 10 for ourselves. Determine the number on the scale we would expect to see for this situation and then rate where we are on the scale. Decide if the number is over or under an expected, typical reaction. Detecting these answers is a next step to overlaying truth on the situation.

Choose it.

Write down a list of *all* the ways you could act based on the detective work done so far. Include actions on this list that appear to be wrong. By doing this, you can see there is *always* a choice in the way you act. Often, people don't see their options and feel trapped or powerless in their situation. You can't always control what happens to you, but there is a lot of opportunity to control how you react. The truth is you can choose to make some terrible decisions, and the fact that you want to choose differently can help provide freedom and healing. After the list is made and all the truth it answers is considered, circle your choice of action or actions on the list.

November 2015, Sarah

*I finally found my husband. We were engaged to be married. However, I still found myself picking fights with him. I would check his phone just to try and catch him in a lie. I would bring up any single thing I could find and start a fight with him. In all my previous relationships, the men had cheated on me. I felt like it was my fault they cheated. **Each time, I pushed my feelings aside and told myself I didn't need anyone.** Now in this relationship, with any little thing that I got frustrated about, I would start a fight. It got so bad that I almost ended the relationship. It wasn't until I* *started to dig a little deeper that I realized I wasn't really frustrated, I was deeply hurt and felt unworthy of his love. Out of this, I began to sabotage my current relationship.*

Feel it.

She was feeling what was happening around and to her in these moments. She noticed frustration and anger. Physically, her heart would beat fast and her hands would tense up. Mentally, she constantly felt not good enough. Relationally, she found herself starting fights.

Name it.

She felt frustrated and angry. After digging a little deeper, it was really hurt and feelings of being unworthy that led her to realize she really felt rejected and lonely.

Truth it.

Her fiancé wasn't cheating. She was having overreactive thoughts. She was experiencing triggers from previous relationships: he wasn't calling after work and wouldn't come home right away, he went and decompressed from work with friends. In her family life growing up, you always checked in. However in his family, you didn't. The wedding was approaching and there were many details to take care, so the stress was also mounting up on her.

Choose it.

She could break off her engagement.

She could trust him.

She could keep sabotaging the relationship and cycle back to this point.

She could do work on her triggers and her negative beliefs about herself, and then see where the relationship was after that.

The follow-up to this story: she ultimately decided to do trauma work on herself and to choose to trust him. They are married now and doing well, always continually working to have a great marriage. She continues to go through the process to really be a detective of her feelings and chooses her actions instead of living out the default reactions.

Often we skip from "Feel it" to "Choose it" and find ourselves suffering because of that. We experience a certain feeling and we react by default. We don't slow the process down to see what else is going on within and around us. We know the "right" truth or we know the "right" behavior to choose, and bypass the other parts of the process. The danger in not slowing the process down is we often miss details that could help us in the future. We create patterns of behavior that are not based on all the facts. We may only know that it is a feeling we may not like, so we choose to do something different in order to avoid having that experience again. Or we don't have the time, so we act in the way we know works and produces the outcome we can live with, even if it's not exactly what we desire. If we jump straight to choosing, we also run the risk of forcing a "right" choice. No matter how right it may seem or how much we *know* it is the best option, we can come to resent it if our feelings aren't caught up with us. In forcing the option we think we *should* choose, we don't get the benefit of working through the feeling. When that feeling comes around again, we repeat the same cycle. The "Choose it" section is meant to be an option we select not out of obligation, but because we have thought about all the options and we intentionally move in a certain direction. When we decide to slow down and figure out what we are feeling, we get different opportunities not otherwise received. We learn more about ourselves and can apply the knowledge to future choices. Chances are that feeling will circle back around at some point, and this time you will be able to discern more specifically what the best choice is based on that recognized feeling and that current situation. We learn our feelings aren't a threat in making bad decisions; rather, they are insights that can lead to intentional choices. We can begin to trust ourselves to process through what we feel instead of shutting ourselves down. We also gain a connection with others when we know more about ourselves and we are able to help others identify their own feelings. Relationships, and from there communities, grow healthier when we choose to do the work on ourselves.

In the example story, she could have been triggered and then jumped straight to a choice that was either negative or positive. Let's say she felt angry and made a choice to forgive him without taking the time to process why she was angry. That choice would have given her the desired outcome of moving on and being okay within the relationship. Yet when that same feeling circles back around and she hasn't done the work of processing what she was really experiencing, she is now left to do the work all over again regardless of her choosing a positive behavior. Or she will be triggered into that feeling again and won't be able to make a choice regarding the specific situation because she will act based on default. She will find herself eventually repeating the same cycle instead of finding freedom through processing. In this story, however, she did choose to slow the process down. In doing this, she gave herself the chance to choose differently from her previous default behavior. From the outside it is clear and easy to say we need to do this, but most of us have similarly experienced the blurriness from the inside of our own story. We need to keep asking ourselves: Why do we feel the way we feel? Or why is this a big deal to me? Or why isn't this a big deal to me? We need to spend some time looking into what is making up the color of our reactions and let our feelings reveal to us what the bigger picture is so we can intentionally choose what to do from that point.

> *Taking the time to slow down the process and ask ourselves some questions can help us navigate a better way to handle feelings rather than to shut down or pretend they don't exist.*

You will begin to see connections and insights that you have never seen before as you take time to allow your mind to go to those hard places. Externalizing, verbal or written, as much of our thought process as we can helps reveal those connections. Our minds want resolution; we want to resolve our negative feelings and repeat the positive ones. The way to get to that is to allow yourself the freedom to go back and process current events, past events, and whatever it is that might have us feeling stuck. Feelings can be complex. A lot is happening in our brains and our bodies when we feel. It can be overwhelming at times, and it can cause us to have default behaviors. Taking the time to slow down the process and ask ourselves some questions can help us navigate a better way to handle feelings rather than to shut down or pretend they don't exist.

Engage

- Think of a previous time when you felt sad, frustrated, angry, embarrassed, etc.
- Go through the Feelings Guide with that experience.
- Feel it.
- Name it.
- Truth it.
- Choose it. (While this experience already happened, list out what your options were at the time and whether or not you would make the same choice now that you have the time to process it again.)

CHAPTER 5

ABLE TO FEEL AGAIN

January 2016, Michael

I knew I didn't feel anything when we talked about your pain. I was watching your face and hearing your words of frustration, but I was so overwhelmed by my own current situation that when we talked, my mind went blank. I can't imagine what it was like for you; I can't even fully figure out what it is like for me. I'm trying to keep my head above water; I am trying to do my job well, to keep my marriage together, to keep my children happy. I'm just trying to survive. I **can't stop to feel and I can't stop to imagine what this is like for you**. *I know I am absent in our relationship, but I can't figure out how to move from where I am now.*

We have now defined "feeling" and "feelings." "Feeling" is the awareness of and experiencing what's happening around you or to you and being conscious of your inner state. "Feelings" are the identified reactions to your feeling; for example, anger, sadness, happiness, etc. If we have found ourselves numb, how do we get back to feeling again? We might have already started the process of feeling again when reading Chapter 4. We might have noticed some feelings as we picked a previous event in which to practice the Feelings Chart. Getting back to feeling may sound like a lot of work. Truthfully it can be, but the good news is it doesn't have to be torturous work. I always remind my clients that they have already survived whatever they are trying to avoid remembering. Whatever the hurt, loss, sadness, anger, or trauma that we have managed to suppress or put on the back burner, we have already lived through and survived it. Even if we are still in the midst of a situation, whatever has happened up until now to cause us to go numb, we have survived it. Remembering it can be painful, but we are in control of how those memories are treated, brought up, and what we do with them. We can do a little at a time easing ourselves into the questions. In therapy, we tell our clients that if they need to shelve something for a bit, they can do that. This is possible when we imagine ourselves putting it into a container and placing it on a shelf. This is not suppressing it because we intend to go back to it and open it up again. There is a vast difference mentally because

> I always remind my clients that they have already survived whatever they are trying to avoid remembering.

we know we aren't ignoring it anymore; instead, we are allowing ourselves boundaries in approaching it. This technique of putting boundaries on our memories and shelving it can be helpful and empowering. We need to give ourselves some grace in this process and know boundaries are okay, and the most important part is to be honest with ourselves through it all.

Two Ways to Feel Again

The first way is through time. Often, we are so busy that we don't stop to reflect on our days or what happened. We get home from work, school, or our activities from the day and the last thing we want to do is to sit and think about all of it. We want to shut down our brains and focus on something else. I have been there and done that, too. However, if this is what we find ourselves doing everyday with no change, being numb will only increase. If we don't give ourselves the opportunity to reflect, we not only miss out on deep joy, but our relationships will suffer as well.

A second way is through empathy. Sometimes looking at someone's story can help us begin to identify our own feelings in a safer, more distant way. We can watch a movie, read a story, or hear from someone we know and start to recognize different feelings. With both of these avenues to feeling again, it is important to externalize our processing. Externalizing, or expressing, is bringing our internal thoughts and putting them into words or pictures and is an important skill that we are able to develop. There are many ways to externalize and we can discover which way works for us. Learning to communicate and externalize our feelings not only helps us individually, it also helps us in our in relationships.

Self-Care

When you are numb, the last thing you may feel like you have energy for is thinking about feelings. I want to encourage you as much as possible to push through that as often as you can and do the work of answering the questions in this book. If you read one part and it sounds too exhausting, skip to another section and go back when you are able. The first section is on time, and that one is probably the most difficult if you are currently numb and lacking the energy to reflect. If you need a break, take one. There really isn't a perfect or a right way to do it. Everyone is different in the ways they begin to feel again. As we read and process and it feels overwhelming on your own, I encourage you to seek a therapist who can help you process. This book is a starting point and some of us have experienced some profound trauma that an outside professional can help us navigate. Identifying the need for help alone can be freeing and healing.

Time

Giving ourselves time and reflecting on feelings can help us to feel again. This might sound so simple, but in looking back at our days and how busy they can be, this can be harder than it seems. We must give ourselves more than five minutes of sitting still, more than a drive with music on, more than a long, overdue shower, more than a 30-minute show on television. No, we must give ourselves real time to reflect. Go for that long drive with no sound but the whirring of the engine. Enjoy that walk alone where you can be intentional with your thoughts. Maybe this is something we used to do more often and have gotten out of the habit of doing, or perhaps we are just starting this practice for the first time, but giving ourselves this time can help to feel again. If we have been numb for a while, or are not used to giving ourselves time, know this can be a practice we can develop. It might be helpful to set a timer if we find ourselves needing to give actual minutes to reflect. Or maybe we already give time to reflect, but we need to focus on quality of time and not the quantity. Perhaps we start out with just a few minutes of intentional time because that is all we can tolerate. As time goes on, we can extend the amount of time, increasing until we are able to reflect as needed. The goal here is to begin to feel again by identifying past or current feelings and building on those. Identifying the last known feeling is a way to narrow down the focus. When trying to find an object you have lost, you attempt to recall the last place you have seen it, and so ask yourself the same question for feeling. Giving ourselves grace and space along the way to do this and increasing the time as we can and as needed. Even if it is in smaller increments, we notice what we are able to and remember that the healthier we get, the healthier our relationships will be with ourselves, others, and God.

Engage

- When do you find yourself practicing the skill of reflection?
- Is the time you spend enough for you?
- Take an inventory of your day. When did you experience feelings?
- What was happening during those moments?

We can build on the skill of reflection from taking a daily inventory as we reflect on more in-depth questions. As we grow in this skill, we are able to see more connections and gain insight. We begin to see the why for how we handled our feelings and where we first started feeling numb in regard to our painful circumstances. It might be as simple as it was too overwhelming in the moment and we shut down; or it might be that we thought we shouldn't feel that way and so we shut down. When we shut down over and over, we start creating a new pattern for ourselves. This pattern leads us to becoming numb. As we learn to recognize this, we give ourselves the chance to make a different choice about how we handle those feelings.

Engage

As you look to this section of Engage, first identify a past time when you remember feeling. Once you have that experience chosen, go through the list of reflection questions. Since you have already been through that situation and have survived, you don't need to shut down the feelings surrounding it. It should be easier to then discover those feelings again, rather than needing to shut them down.

When was the last time I felt anger, sadness, or hurt either about a specific situation or in general?

Follow the Feelings Guide for that situation:

<u>Feel it.</u>

- How would you describe the physical feelings of anger, sadness, or hurt?

<u>Name it.</u>

- What feeling comes up as you describe the physical sensations?

<u>Truth it.</u>

- Do those feelings seem appropriate for the situation?
- What was happening that made those feelings arise?
- Can you remember the details around it?
- What people were there, or were you by yourself?
- What was the weather like that day?
- What events were going on with you?
- Was it a single event or multiple events that happened?
- What happened in the following days?
- Was it a slow, over-time trauma, or did it happen on a particular day?
- Were there multiple events that led to those feelings?

<u>Choose it.</u>

- What did I do with those feelings?
- What choices did I make?
- Did this lead to me becoming numb?

When was the last time I felt extreme joy, excitement, happiness, or gratitude either about a specific situation or in general? Follow the Feelings Guide for that situation:

Feel it.

- How would you describe the physical feelings of anger, sadness, or hurt?

Name it.

- What feeling comes up as you describe the physical sensations?

Truth it.

- Do those feelings seem appropriate for the situation?
- What was happening that made those feelings arise?
- Can you remember the details around it?
- What people were there, or were you by yourself?
- What was the weather like that day?
- What events were going on with you?
- Was it a single event or multiple events that happened?
- What happened in the following days?
- Was it a slow, over-time trauma, or did it happen on a particular day?
- Were there multiple events that led to those feelings?

Choose it.

- What did I do with those feelings? What choices did I make?

Below are some story examples of a person going through this notes section. From here, you can begin to connect to your feelings by becoming aware again of the physical signs, the details around the feeling, and the choice you made during that time. You might have trained your brain to stopped processing feelings, but your body can still recall physical sensations if you give it some time and space to do that. Identifying the answers to these questions and what was happening when you felt those feelings can help connect you back to feeling.

November 2015, Mia

*I watched the Publix commercial on TV of a family celebrating Thanksgiving together and **I cried, but not a normal "that's so sweet" cry**, but a longing-for-what-was-happening cry. I don't know why. I have a good family. I am married with two great kids. I have a relationship with my mom and dad and sisters. It's fine. I'm fine.*

- When was the last time I felt anger, sadness, hurt either about a specific situation or in general?

  The last time I felt a real sadness, a deep sadness or rather, hurt, about my family was in high school. My dad was always working and never came home.

- What was happening that made those feelings arise? Do those feelings seem appropriate for the situation?

  The way I cried at a Publix commercial doesn't seem like it was appropriate for the situation. But seeing that family together in a warm way made me cry.

- How would you describe the physical feelings of anger, sadness, or hurt?

  I feel it in my gut, like, my stomach hurts. And my heart pounds because I am mad. I kind of want to just run.

- What did I do with those feelings?

  I pushed them away. He was working to provide for us. He needed to do that and it needed to be okay with me. It wasn't even a conversation we had, so I would just distract myself and move on from it.

October 2015, Kay

I don't feel joy anymore. *I look at my kids and my husband and feel nothing. I use to be able to see their smiles and just feel overwhelmed with joy. Now it is gone.*

- When was the last time I felt extreme joy, excitement, happiness, or gratitude either about a specific situation or in general?

  The last time I felt extreme joy was when I found out I was pregnant.

- What was happening that made those feelings arise? Do those feelings seem appropriate for the situation?

  We had been desiring another child for quite some time and so to find out that I was pregnant was amazing. I do think the feeling then matched the situation. But seeing my family's faces now and having no reaction doesn't match how I know I feel.

- How would you describe the physical feelings of joy, happiness, excitement, or gratitude?

  My heart feels full, I get a little teary-eyed, and I want to jump.

- What did I do with those feelings?

  When I miscarried, I crashed. So all those feelings of joy disappeared. I forgot what it was like when I found out I was pregnant with the other two kids and the pleasure of carrying them in me and holding them as newborns. But I remember now the joy of seeing my firstborn's little face as he was swaddled in a blanket. It makes my heart swell again.

From the outside, the connections between what happened and why these feelings are absent may seem obvious. Discovering these connections can help us to get unstuck and to feel again. When we continually push feelings away and move on, we deprive ourselves of seeing the connections. Oftentimes in therapy, I share with people a connection I observe as they begin to share their story. I notice how it makes sense for the way they feel because of what they just described to me. The lightbulb goes off and they see it for themselves. This happens when they offer themselves the time to process and reflect on intentional questions. We then talk about, or externalize, the connection and they can begin to intentionally choose what they want to do from there.

Empathy

There are multiple ways to get back to feeling. That's good news if we have been numb for a while and it is difficult to feel again: we can use these tools individually or combine them. Empathy can be another tool to feeling again. Accessing other's situations and feeling for them might be an easier way back to feeling. It can be less overwhelming and more controlled and, therefore, an emotionally safer approach.

Empathy, like feelings, does not have one universal definition. There are multiple definitions: feeling another's feelings, understanding another's feelings, or acting in a way that shows you understand another's feelings. While these are different definitions, I think these are all aspects of empathy. Daniel Goleman, author of *Emotional Intelligence and Social Intelligence*, recalls a conversation with Paul Ekman where Ekman shared his thoughts on three types of empathy. (http://www.danielgoleman.info/three-kinds-of-empathy-cognitive-emotional-compassionate/) One type is "cognitive empathy: simply knowing how the other person feels and what they might be thinking." He also referred to this as perspective-taking empathy. A second type is "emotional empathy: when you feel physically along with the other person, as though their emotions were contagious." Lastly, the third type, "compassionate empathy: we not only understand a person's predicament and feel with them, but are spontaneously moved to help, if needed."

We continue to see there are many ways to think about empathy, and maybe one of those definitions is how we have defined and lived it out. To get us all on the same page moving forward, and if we are to use empathy as a tool in feeling again, we need to have a common working definition here. In this book, we will define empathy as the understanding and sharing of another's feelings and experiences. For clarification in our definition, sharing doesn't mean owning their feelings or experiences; rather, engaging in them with another person.

Empathy can be a way back to feeling and come back from being numb. Sometimes it feels impossible to think about someone else and what a situation is like for them, yet practicing the skill of empathy can be the best prescription for getting back to any kind of feeling. If we define feeling as the awareness of what's happening around or to you, and feelings as the reaction to that, then what better way to access our own feelings than becoming more aware of others around us? We can get over-whelmed in thinking about our personal life and trying to feel again, so let's simply start the process by entering another door such as empathy.

Engage

- What has been your definition of empathy?
- In what ways do you consider yourself empathic?
- Can you think of a time when you were numb and had a hard time being empathic?

Ways to grow in the skill of empathy:

1. Affect:

    - Looking at a person's affect is a useful technique because it teaches us to notice cues that are in our everyday world. Affect is the display of feelings through facial expressions, hand gestures, tone of voice, or other body language. When teaching about feelings, we identify what a person might be experiencing based on their outward affect. For those of us wanting to grow our empathy skill, this is a great place to start. Notice others around you, their affect, and their other nonverbal communication of feelings. Of course we won't always know the story of what is going on, but we can begin to imagine what it might be like to understand and share in those feelings.

HOW DO YOU FEEL TODAY?

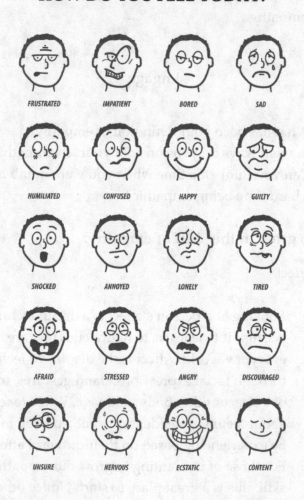

This is an affect of feelings chart. The chart is used for a client who might have difficulty putting into words what feeling it is they are experiencing. They can point out the picture of affect that resonates with what is happening inside them. It connects what is happening on the outside to what is happening on the inside. We might have stopped feeling for so long that we have trouble naming our own feelings. This chart or something similar can help with that. Beginning to determine what you are feeling based on detecting another's perceived feeling is a great first step to feeling again.

This chart can also be used to identify affect, the way a feeling is expressed on our faces. We might point to the sad face and ask a client to identify the specific feeling. We then ask *why* might this person be feeling that way. In other words, what led them to this affect. For example, let's say we point to the face that has a frown and a tear. The client would identify that as sad. We ask the client to explain the why behind that feeling. The why that is said is typically a personal experience that has made them sad or a concrete example of a story they know that caused sadness. While adults have many stories they can name as a possible why, even child clients are able to do this activity. They might say: mommy went away and didn't come back for a long time; someone took their favorite toy; they fell and got a boo-boo. Through connecting a story to an affect, we learn the skill of relating to others and having empathy. We can begin to connect how another person would feel sad in a particular situation and we can share in those feelings. We can learn to empathize and make connections that help us to feel again.

Engage

- When was the last time you noticed someone with a sad affect or happy affect?
- What do you think they were experiencing? What is a possible why for this affect?
- What kind of experience would cause you to have that affect in your own life?

2. Movie scenarios:

- Another way to learn and practice empathy is to watch a movie that we know will typically elicit different kinds of feelings. This one can be helpful because we have the scene and the why laid out for us. We might be able to enter it more easily than connecting to a stranger's affect. In the movie, we get to "know" a character; we learn about them and we see their story unfold. In the same way affect works, we can connect to the story through empathy.

Engage

Think of a recent movie that leaned more toward the drama category. (Or choose a movie, watch it, and answer the questions as an actual exercise.)

- Are you able to feel for a character?
- Can you imagine yourself in their situation?
- Are they sad, angry, excited, happy, etc.?
- Are you able to connect what is happening on the outside (their story) to what is happening on the inside (your story)?
- How are you understanding and sharing in the feelings they are showing?

3. Friend/Acquaintance:

- The most realistic and close to home example is when a friend or acquaintance is sharing their story with us. We know this person and might have experienced other journeys with them already. This could be more helpful in getting to empathy, or this could make it harder to have empathy. For some of us, knowing the person can make it too overwhelming, and we will shut down. If we are able to stay engaged with the person and have true empathy, then we can take that opportunity to connect to our own feelings. Everyone is different in how we can connect and have empathy. Starting to feel again may take a few tries and some different attempted avenues.

Engage

Think of a friend who has recently gone through an event that elicited strong feelings—whether happy or sad.

- What happens when a friend or someone you know begins to tell you a story about their life that has been or is really challenging or exciting? Do you disconnect in the conversation? Are you able to engage and share in it with them?
- Have there been previous events where your reactions were different when they shared a story like this one with you?
- How are you curious about how they handled or are handling it, or what it was like for them in the different parts of the story?
- Can you identify if they are angry, sad or happy, excited, or many feelings at one time? Can you identify why they feel that way?
- Can you imagine yourself in that story and how you would feel?

4. Serving

- From this place of empathy, we can also serve others. This goes back to sharing in another's feelings or experiences. Sharing can be tangible. Serving others allows us the time and distance we might need from our own processing as well.

We can learn the needs of others and serve them, which requires our focus to shift intentionally from our story to theirs for a time. We can send a text message, make a meal, send a gift card for groceries, or mow a yard for someone in need. Sometimes we just need to look around us. Seeing other people's situations and how they are feeling can help us find our own healing. As we begin to empathize and serve, we begin to feel more and experience more. It's at this time that our feelings start to move beyond just "fine" to feeling even deeper joy once again.

Engage

- What stories have you heard shared recently?
- Identify a person in your life whom you can serve.
- List the ways that story would be hard or difficult to endure.
- What would help you if that were your story? Would that be a way that they would feel served too?
- What is the best way you can serve them? (encouragement, a meal, giving money, a card, mowing their lawn, getting groceries for them)
- Do it!

The overlap between these tools is to externalize what we are experiencing. In this book, we see this as a common thread in each section. From answering questions in the notes sections to naming our feelings, it is important to get out of our head and externalize what is happening.

Externalizing

One day my daughter, who was a toddler at the time, was crying in the car because one of her toys fell on the floor and I couldn't reach it to pick it up. I made attempts to comfort her and let her know I would get it for her as soon as I could. She wouldn't stop crying and I said, "Okay, okay, enough crying—I will get it when I can," and she screamed through her tears, "I just wanna cry!" A lesson for me, even after all these years of encouraging others just to feel, was that my daughter was expressing her feelings and I needed to let her. We sometimes encourage our kids, friends, and ourselves to shut down feelings and just move on. Learning to process or externalize our feelings is a skill. It is a skill that, unfortunately, not many people are taught in childhood or adolescence. Instead, we hear statements like, "Don't cry," "You're fine," "Suck it up," "There's no need to cry about that," or "Just move on." These come from trusted people in our lives, either authority figures or friends. Before we know it, this behavior of not expressing ourselves is praised and reinforced by statements like "You're so strong" and "Wow, you didn't even cry"; and we now have the skill of suppressing our feelings instead of processing them. We will either learn to suppress our feelings or we can learn to express our feelings—all of them. When we talk about feelings, it's often the negative ones that receive the most attention. However, externalizing means also being able to recognize and communicate gratefulness, joy, happiness, surprise, love, etc., in addition to the negative ones.

Being able to express or externalize our feelings is one aspect of a popular researched topic called emotional intelligence. While there is ongoing empirical research being done on emotional intelligence, one of the more comprehensive working definitions is it's "a set of abilities (verbal and nonverbal) that enable a person to generate, recognize, express, understand and evaluate their own and others' emotions in order to guide thinking and action and successfully cope with environmental demands and pressures." (Van Rooy DL, Viswesvaran C. Emotional intelligence: A meta-analytic investigation of predictive validity and nomological net. J Vocat Behav 2004; 65:71–95) Peter Salovey and Jack Meyer, who first coined the term 'emotional intelligence' in 1990, believe that "some people are innately more emotionally intelligent than others. However, people can develop emotional intelligence, particularly at critical periods including infancy and teenage years." (http://www.journeytoexcellence.org.uk/resourcesandcpd/research/summaries/rsemotionalintelligence.asp) This is good news because it means that all of us can gain the skill of processing and expressing our feelings and emotions. This skill can be developed and built up as we learn. We can pass this skill to others as well.

As we start to grow in this skill, there are some tangible ways to get us started. If we struggle with putting our feelings into words and we can't quite describe it yet, writing down our thoughts is a great place to start. Maybe we don't know how we feel yet, but we know we are upset or not happy. Simply write that thought down and give yourself some time to reflect on it. Or perhaps we had a bad day and we start externalizing by listing the facts or events that happened that day. From there we take that list and we can recognize where we started feeling bad about the day. Externalizing through writing allows us to express, understand, and evaluate our feelings and see them in a different way.

The following are some ways to tangibly and practically externalize and process what you're feeling:

Follow the Feelings Guide: Feel it, Name it, Truth it, Choose it (See Chapter 4).

- Are you glad, sad, mad, frustrated, disappointed, surprised, grateful, angry? Writing it down will help you process and externalize it. Slowing the process down to really make it a conscious choice grows this intelligence.

Journal: (write down) or draw from that feeling place

- Write down your answers in the Notes sections of this book.
- What words describe the feeling in your body? How would you describe the event that led to those feelings? What other feelings come about because of it? Why do you think you feel that way? What do you want to do with those feelings?

- What pictures come to your mind? What illustrates the feeling? What colors would you use to describe it? Why do you think you feel that way? What is the picture that you want with those feelings?
- Stream of consciousness also works here because sometimes we just need to sit and see what comes up for us. Don't box yourself into rules for how it should look or be, just write or draw.
- Journaling doesn't need to be organized. It can be bullet points or just a word, or even just a thought.

Talking to a trusted person

- Describe verbally what is going on, what feelings you have, or what you have experienced. Simply talking in itself is externalizing.
- Sometimes walking and talking (or any shared activity) can help us think through what we want to say and is a little less intimidating than just sitting across from someone and sharing all of our internal thoughts.

Talk to a professional counselor

- Sometimes we need to go to a person outside of our life. One of the most beneficial parts of therapy is telling your story to someone who doesn't know it. They hear and observe experiences and feelings that can be valuable to your own processing. They can ask questions that others who are in your story won't ask because either others assume they know the answer or they won't want to ask you a particular question. This form of externalizing and processing can be advantageous.

Intentionally bringing up the feeling helps get us focused on what is happening to us at that moment. Journaling or drawing is a way to get those feelings outside of our heads and into something tangible. Often, we can ruminate about an individual event or thought, and simply "getting it out" can help us process and see it in a new way. It can help clear our minds a little bit more so we can let truth enter in, or think about it in a new light. Likewise, talking to a trusted person is also helpful. A trusted person can listen while we talk and process what is happening, or ask questions to help us understand more about why we are feeling the way we are feeling. It is essential to choose a person who can listen well and is trusted by us when using the talking option. Surprisingly, many people don't have the skill to listen well. Although their intentions are good, they focus on trying to solve your problem or being the answer for us. They tend to project by interjecting their own experiences and making them identical to ours. They aren't able to handle our feelings, so they might cut us off with one of the earlier statements like, "It will all be okay." On the other hand, people who listen well do the following: listen with their body language, don't need to have an answer for us, empathize without projecting, and ask questions in a curious way about what is happening with us. Before we share with a person, we need to make sure they are trusted and can listen in the ways described. I have found that when listening well and asking questions, the clients or friends come up with a better thought than I could have. I can't assume I know the right answer, have the best approach, or know precisely what they are going through, so instead I listen well and hope that together in a conversation they find some truth or simply clear their minds through talking. We can all be that trusted person who can listen well to our friends.

It might take a few different tries at the different approaches to figure out which one suits us best. For me, it can be a mixture. Sometimes it is journaling, where I write and process; other times, I go for a walk with my husband and we talk and process together. My husband likes to draw in his journal and makes a visual picture of what he is processing. Everyone is different and every situation can be different too. I've also sought out professional help for when it was too overwhelming for me and it wasn't getting better. Being honest with ourselves and asking the questions that we have gone through in this chapter on a regular basis can help us know where to go and what to try so that we can begin to feel again. It is a process, and it is important to give yourself some grace and patience to figure it out and try different ways.

Learning different ways to externalize how we are feeling can help us as we seek to express and communicate what's been internalized.

Getting back to feeling can be work, but there are different ways to access those feelings. Giving ourselves time to reflect can offer some insight on how to get unstuck from where we are numb. Maybe an easier route would be to access those feelings from the place of empathy. Looking at someone's affect or listening to a friend's story and understanding as well as sharing in their feelings and experiences. Through empathy, we can begin to see the connections and from there start to see or recognize our own feelings again. Learning different ways to externalize how we are feeling can help us as we seek to express and communicate what's been internalized. All these ways help us start to add different colors around the color white, add feelings around our numb, so that we can begin to feel again.

CHAPTER 6

How to Prevent
Feeling Numb

August, 2013, Kay

I was so excited to tell my family that I was finally pregnant again. I couldn't wait to share the news I had kept a surprise for twelve weeks. They were so excited when I called and told them and they saw the ultrasound picture of our healthy baby. In that same conversation, my mom shared with me that she hadn't been feeling great and was going in for another colonoscopy in another week. She told me not to worry, that it could be anything, and she would keep us updated. Two weeks later we found out my mom had colon cancer. **The feelings of numb seemed to be just around the corner again.**

Once we have started on the journey back to feeling again, it is important to continue to give ourselves time to check in with all that's going on in our lives. It is also significant to see how each chapter builds on the one before it. It might seem to repeat, but each chapter is designed to give a new foundation block and make sure the block under it is strong. There is overlapping information and concepts that will shape how, and if, we move forward. I have been numb and I know that our foundations can feel a little shaky when we are in that place. It is vital we know why and how we are rebuilding and what to do moving forward.

As we choose to live in this way, the next building block is to be disciplined about living in what I call the "Zoom-in/Zoom-out" life. It's a way to live with a balanced perspective. Zoom-in to check in on the details of what is happening daily and zoom-out to get a better view of the big picture. Like a camera shows you different images based on whether you are zoomed-in or zoomed-out, we need to do the same with our own lives.

The zoomed-in photograph of the leaf shows the many details that we need. We can't live in just the bigger picture because we miss the important building blocks of who we are and how we have gotten to this place in our lives. In the zoomed-in photo, we see the cells that make up the leaf. If we didn't have those specific details, we wouldn't have the leaf; and without the leaves, there is no beautiful big tree. Likewise, the zoomed-out photo of a big beautiful tree is full of those detailed leaves. We can't live in just the details because there is always so much more going on with us, the whole picture of how each part has made this giant fantastic picture. It gives perspective and a chance for truth to enter in a way we might not have been able to hear it before. It helps us remain healthy enough to hear the truth because we are not staying so stagnant in our lives that the good things can't enter. We start to see colors close up and then how those blend of colors make an incredible story. In that constant zoom-in/zoom-out perspective, we can stay balanced about what is going on in and around us. The balance helps us not to concentrate so overwhelmingly on one part that we become numb. Switching between them allows us to zoom-in and focus on the pain, hurt, sadness or disappointment, and to zoom-out to receive a different perspective and a holistic view of our life.

It is not possible to experience a time when the zoom-in and zoom-out pictures are the same. They offer two different views, and living with that parallel view can be healthy and helpful. There are times when much happens in every aspect of our life that it feels like those pictures are the same, yet the zoom-out picture will always include everything we have already made it through. It will show us the other hard places, survival moments, and celebrations that make up who we are as a person. Think back to a time where it felt like life would never be different from it was at that moment. Zoom in. Maybe we thought a relationship would never be healed or perhaps that baby would never come, or there would be no relief in our finances or we would always be in that job. Zoom out. Look at life now. Is that circumstance still the same? What's different now? Life ebbs and flows; circumstances that feel like they last forever can be overwhelming to the point that we shut down. Choosing to see both pictures and doing the work of staying engaged will help us not to go numb.

We always have choices. We can control the amount of time we spend in each picture. The zoomed-in picture might, at times, feel overwhelming. We can let ourselves slowly enter into the details of what is happening and for a shorter amount of time if needed. After doing that for a while, the time we can spend zoomed-in might get longer. From there we start to reflect on those details, ask and honestly answer questions about it. The zoomed-in questions are similar to what we did in Chapter 5 as we learned to begin to feel again. Zoom-in is giving ourselves that time to reflect. It is using that technique that we now do on a more regular basis and incorporating it into our view and balancing it with the zoom-out perspective. Zoom-out questions include remembering when we have been in this place before, asking what happened then, and seeing how it added to our tree and shaped us. Zoom-out asks how we survived it before and what is different now with this situation; it gives us the chance to see a bigger picture.

Engage

Zoom-In Questions

- What am I feeling today?
- Has anything happened today or this week that has made me feel sad, angry, frustrated, happy, joyful, or disappointed?
- Is there anything ongoing that is contributing to how I am feeling either negatively or positively?

Zoom-Out Questions

- When have I been here before?
- What happened then?
- Where am I going and how will this help me?

October 2016, Kay

*We moved, and we have debt all over again. **I am frustrated and
concerned** that we are not going to be able to make it.*

Zoom-In

- What am I feeling today? Has anything happened
  today or this week that has made me feel sad, angry,
  frustrated, happy, joyful, disappointed? Is there
  anything ongoing that is contributing to how I am
  feeling, either negatively or positively?

  *I am feeling anger that we are in this place again. It feels
  overwhelming to me. We worked so hard to get out of it the
  first time, and now we are back to barely covering all of our
  bills. I am sad that a job hasn't worked out for me yet here.
  Ongoing, I feel responsible for not adding to the family
  income and also really upset that I had to leave my job when
  we moved.*

Zoom-Out

- When have I been here before? What happened then?
  Where am I going and how will this help me?

  *We have been in this place before, but it was even worse
  then. We climbed our way out of debt little by little with
  God's help. I know this is a season, and I will be able to work
  again eventually. During this season, I have been able to take*

care of my mom who was sick and be home with my daughter who hasn't started school yet.

We can see when we zoom in there are a lot of appropriate feelings going on there. However, that's not the whole picture. There are other parts at work at the same time. When we zoom out, the bigger picture gives the perspective that it's not going to last forever and there was good coming out this time of hardship. One perspective doesn't negate the other one. We can feel both grateful and sad at the same time. We can feel both frustrated and hopeful at the same time. They can both be true to what's going on in our life. Perspective and balance of where we are placing our focus matters.

> *Perspective and balance of where we are placing our focus matters.*

Adding the building block of zoom-in and zoom-out helps us to stay in feeling. We are able to choose how much time we spend in each picture. We can zoom in to reflect and spend time identifying what is happening in and around us at this given point in time. There might be a great deal of events that are causing us to feel overwhelmed and want to shut down feeling altogether. Then we can switch to the zoom-out picture of our lives. We discover hope in that we can thrive in this time as we see how previous life events have made our tree bigger and stronger than it was before.

CHAPTER 7

RELATIONAL IMPACT

October 2008, Matt

My adoptive mom had just passed away. I felt like I wanted to finally search for my biological mother. I never wanted to do it before, but now the timing seemed right for me. I wasn't sure what to do or how to feel about it all. I was grieving my mom, but at the same time trying to figure out how to feel about possibly finding my bio mother. I felt confused but pushed ahead. About a month later, I found out my biological mother had passed a few years earlier. **Now I am left with trying to figure out how to grieve a relationship I won't ever have.**

Relationships start the moment we are born. Before we can even choose to have them in our life, the relationships with our biological mother and biological father are present even if we never meet them. The relationships we have in life exist from the time we are born, through growing up, to being an adult, and at the end of life. Whether or not you are engaged in those relationships is different from recognizing that they exist. Many different relationships will enter your life. There are the deep, nurturing relationships and the ones you superficially encounter; the ones who love you well and the ones who don't.

Relationships can provide a temperature reading of what is going on around us. When others are feeling deeply about an event and we have no feeling, we can pay attention to something we might have otherwise missed. When we notice a lack of trusted people in our lives, we can discover why. When we identify a pattern repeating with a certain person in our lives, we learn to break the cycle. Relationships offer insight and help us to ask questions about ourselves and what we believe. We uncover the trusted relationships that can help us find freedom and healing.

To have the healthiest relationships, we must be the healthiest version of ourselves.

Relationships exist for everyone, and they are present in our everyday lives. What those and other relationships look like as we get older depends on us. To have a healthiest relationships, we must be the healthiest version of ourselves. An article put out by the American Public Health Association (4) says, "Without question, the mental health of all parties is the most important element of a good relationship." While we cannot control whether or not the other person in the relationship is healthy, we can control how healthy we are and what we are contributing to make it a good relationship. A big part of feeling numb is the sense of no connection to feelings and therefore our potential loss of connection to people, events, and the details of our life. In that "fine" place, we not only miss out on the depth of feelings, but we also miss out on the depth of connection happening around us. Being numb bleeds into each of our interactions and affects all of our relationships. We may think we are able to turn it off or on, but in reality it cannot be contained or compartmentalized. Rediscovering our feelings will also help us rediscover those connections. Those connections will lead us to being the healthiest version of ourselves and having healthier relationships. As each increases, it in turn grows the other. We become healthier individuals through our relationships, and our relationships become healthier—making us an even healthier version of ourselves.

Self-Care

Being numb can affect your memories as well. If you notice that you have blocks of time where you have no memory or they are blank and there is no medical reason for it, pay attention to that. Trauma that leads to being numb can also block you from connection to certain memories. While this serves you during the traumatic times by helping you to survive, there is a time where you are once again safe enough to process that. If this is where you find yourself, I would again encourage professional counseling to help with this part of the process.

Sometimes we can find ourselves shutting down the feeling intentionally because a relationship in our life is the situation in which we are numb. What if we are numb in a relationship because of the relationship? What if it's too painful to feel a betrayal or it's been so long with the same hurt happening over and over again? What are we to do with that?

March 2014 - A friendship

*I realized that she unfriended me in every sense of the word used today. We used to be so close—having lunch once a week and texting throughout our days. We intentionally connected on what was happening in our lives. Our husbands were even closer and our kids were best friends; each person longed to spend time with their counterpart. When I began to reach out to talk or have lunch and receive no reply, I knew something was wrong. She finally told me that I wasn't allowed in her life anymore, and it hurt deeply. I asked what the offense was and was told there wasn't one. I would follow up with another question seeking an explanation but was given none. When I continually tried to contact her, I was met with continued silence. I was so confused; I was just cut out. I tried to stay in the relationship and not just run away, but this kept going and continues still. **I can't feel mad or sad all the time**, so I go numb.*

September 2012 - A marriage

We've been fighting for years it seems. There are moments here and there that are okay, but somehow the same fight keeps coming up. We have been through some difficult times, and we made it through *those, but it seems there are places still that neither of us will change. We try to resolve it, but sometimes we just come to an impasse and then just get so tired that we just stop talking for a bit. I try so hard to stay engaged in this marriage, yet I find that **I can't just feel this deeply for so long**. It's exhausting.*

July 2016 - A parent

*My mom has so many feelings that it isn't safe for me to have mine. I don't know how to talk to her about it because she's my mom, the adult. So instead **I don't talk about how I feel**. I just move on. I find myself taking care of her and shutting down completely.*

Within relationships, we can practice the zoom-in/zoom-out technique that we learned in Chapter 6.

Zoom in. Recognize and name the feelings we are having in the moment we think about the relationship. Think about why they are there and determine what is contributing to those strong feelings. Identify the specific circumstances surrounding this relationship that led to those feelings. Maybe we discover we are numb in the relationship. Consider what led us to feeling numb within this relationship. If we find we are numb, we can revisit chapters 4 and 5 to process those feelings and focus on ourselves within this relationship.

Zooming in can also bring up parts of the relationship we might need to grieve or forgive. It can shine light on the details we might otherwise have missed. Sometimes a relationship changes or ends, and we need to grieve that loss. There is a section on actively grieving in the end of this chapter for a more in-depth way of working through grief. Often we discount the need to grieve a person or a change within a relationship because we minimize the hurt, or we place an expectation on ourselves to be "fine." Perspective is helpful, but if a hurt is upsetting us, then we need to pay attention to that before we can simply move on from it. Forgiveness acts in a similar way. If we feel hurt by the other person then, by definition, the need for forgiveness is there. (For more on forgiveness, see Chapter 8) Both grief and forgiveness impact our relationships and whether or not we go numb.

Sustaining hurt requires energy and time, and we don't have enough energy or time to consistently live in the hurt. We can process whatever is externalized, but we can't process that which we are keeping internalized. If we don't name the hurt we have experienced or what is happening relative to this relationship, we will shut down over time. Externalizing and naming the hurt can be processed through the Feelings Guide exercise, journaling/drawing, talking to a trusted friend or a professional counselor. Whether the need is to grieve, forgive, or grieve and forgive, we are in control of where we choose to focus and what we decide to do in the relationship.

Zoom out. Zooming out on a relationship can be hard because the hurt wants to keep us in it. Because hurt demands our full attention, it makes it easier to stay there and difficult to zoom out. The zoom-out perspective allows us to answer questions about whether or not the healthiest versions of people are present. While no one is ever perfectly healthy, there are times when we are going through difficulties and aren't able to offer what another person might need. We need to recognize that the other person (or us) might not be in a place to engage in this relationship. It has been said, "Hurt people hurt people." Hurting people, not choosing to change, is another example of a negative cycle. When we don't do the work of being the healthiest version of ourselves, we can't engage fully in relationships; when we can't engage fully in relationships, we can't become the healthiest version of ourselves; the cycle continues on until we decide to do something differently from before.

While zoomed out, we also have the opportunity to identify if unhealthy patterns are showing up for either ourselves or the other person. Maybe there is a pattern of shutting down internally, showing aggression, or avoiding confrontation when there is conflict. Do we see these relationship patterns in our own life or the other person? If the other person is displaying these patterns, we need to allow ourselves not to take it personally even if everything they are doing is personal. We must remember that we can't change the other person. We can only change what we do. If we see unhealthy patterns in our other relationships, we can take that as an opportunity to dig a little deeper into what is happening within ourselves. It can be difficult to identify patterns in our own life. If we are unsure they exist, we can seek feedback from a trusted person. Gaining insight helps us move forward, see the broader picture, and control what we can change. When we decide to change within a relationship,

When we decide to change within a relationship, the relationship will change.

the relationship will change. That truth should be encouraging and empowering for us as we navigate relationships.

Another aspect of the zoomed-out perspective is to ask the question, what good can you see coming from what is presently happening. Often when we run into deep hurts, seeing good is hard. However, your suffering doesn't have to be the end of the story; there can be more. It is one of the best zoom-out questions you can ask yourself. The hurt itself isn't good but, from pain, we often move to another place in our life. If we make healthy choices, we move to a healthier place. Experiencing a forward shift will never make what happened good, but if we are looking at the broader picture, we can see the overall positive effect. One healthy difference can change the zoomed-out picture. Perspective and balance of where you are placing your focus matters.

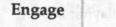

Engage

Zoom-In

- Recognize the feelings you have, why they are there, and what is currently happening to keep those feelings strong.
- Grieve what has happened in this relationship and what you used to have with that person before this hurt.
- Forgive if there is hurt you need to forgive.
- Reflect on what you could do better or could have done better during each step.

Zoom-Out

- Is this person healthy enough to be in this relationship right now?
- Are you healthy enough to be in this relationship right now?
- Are there other relationships in my life or the other person's life where this is happening?
- Is there a pattern of some sort that I can recognize, either in my life or the other person's?
- What good can I see coming from this?

Friendship example:

Zoom-In

I feel so sad because I miss my friend. I am angry because I can't even have a conversation to talk about what happened. Despite the fact that I keep trying to reach out, I just get ignored.

I know I need to grieve our friendship, so I often look at pictures of times we used to spend together and journal about past experiences we had. I also wrote her a letter, which I didn't send, to reminisce and be thankful for all the time we had until this. I also know I need to forgive her. I need to forgive each thing that I find myself holding onto from all of this hurt.

Zoom-Out

I know she has a lot of past experiences and trauma that don't help her have healthy relationships. So I know there is healing that needs to happen and this isn't just affecting me.

I feel like I'm in a good place. I have asked for feedback from two trusted people on how I am handling this and letting me know if at any point I sound unhealthy.

There are other relationships in her life right now that aren't going well, too.

I know she tends to shut people out or just move on from situations and people quickly. For me, I see that I care a lot about what their perception is of me and others whom they might be talking to about what is happening. So I am working on telling myself truth and being okay with that being enough; and living in that especially right now when I can't control or fix anything. And not being able to control or fix it is also very hard for me.

I can see that sometimes our friendship could have been unhealthy. I know that my friend and her husband were close to us and because of that, sometimes decisions could be made based on those friendships instead of being free to do what each family needed to do. Having that separation in some ways has been helpful.

Parent example:

Zoom-In

I am beyond being mad at my mom. I am just sad that I don't have a real relationship with her, and I don't see how one can happen now. I need to grieve all the lost time with her over these last years. I am almost eighteen now and can see how I didn't really have a mom to talk to in my teenage years. It makes me deeply sad to look back and see what I missed. I also see other moms of my friends and wish that I could talk to my mom the way they talk to their moms. I know I need to forgive her. I am working on that, even though it feels continual. I think instead I just act like everything is okay, because that seems easier.

Zoom-Out

I can see my mom has some past hurt that she needs to deal with and that puts up walls in our relationship. But I can't say if my mom is healthy enough to have a relationship with me, it would feel weird to say that. I can see in my other relationships that I have started to shut down in those too. The difference is I feel like those people are safe enough for me to talk to and say what I need to say. I can see where I have become numb because of my relationship with my mom. So I could probably start opening up more to the people I know are safe for me, even those moms whom my friends talk to as well. Maybe if I can be less numb, I can talk to my mom more too.

If we choose to dwell on the hurt and live in unforgiveness, the only way to ultimately sustain that is to shut down and become numb. From there, we become bitter and miss out on life. We miss out on other current relationships and feeling deep joy. We miss out on growing our character and learning how to cope in better ways. We may even miss out on new relationships we could have had. On the other hand, if we choose to look at what we can change in ourselves and seek the good coming from the hurt, we can stay engaged and not become numb. The more healthy choices we make to zoom in, to recognize our

Loss is a common experience that can be encountered many times during a lifetime; it does not discriminate.

feelings, to regulate them and react, the more the zoom-out picture becomes full and clear and our perspective is balanced.

Grieving

As we zoom in, we might discover there might be some time we need to give ourselves to grieve. Grieving is a term we hear often. Simply, it's when we experience a loss. We are deprived of, or there is a removal of someone or something of great value. It could be someone or something that has enriched our life in a meaningful way, or it could be time invested in someone or something. Loss is a common experience that can be encountered many times during a lifetime; it does not discriminate. Everyone endures loss. One can experience multiple secondary losses at the same time from the same situation. For example, someone going through a divorce has lost their spouse, perhaps their home, time with their children, decrease in financial support, time with friends or family, and the list can go on. Some of these losses are tangible and some are symbolic, yet no less painful and difficult.

Grieving is hard. Lack of understanding makes it harder.

How do we know if we are grieving or adjusting to loss? We are feeling it. People who are enduring loss or are grieving say it can feel like you have been weighed down and aged twenty years overnight. It can be as simple as not feeling like ourselves. Or it can be more complex and we may not have the same amount of energy or desires as we did before; or we may feel anxious, sad, or depressed. We may see it in our behavior as lacking attention or unable to sit still. Socially, we withdraw from friends and activities; physically we cry, have sleep disturbances, or our eating habits change; cognitively, we may discover negative self-judgments or preoccupation with thoughts of that person, object, or dream. Whether we see grief in our lives socially, emotionally, or mentally, it's our body's natural ability to heal our emotional injury. It allows us to know that something isn't quite right, and we need to pay attention to that. Grieving is hard. Lack of understanding makes it harder.

Self-Care

If you find that you are grieving and if it feels overwhelming, please seek out a professional counselor to help you navigate this season.

"The quickest way for anyone to reach the sun and the light of day is not to run west, chasing after the setting sun, but to head east, plunging into the darkness until one comes to the sunrise."

(Gerald L. Sittser, *A Grace Disguised: How the Soul Grows through Loss*)

Sometimes we need to sit in the darkness for a bit and wait for the sunrise. The more natural thing to do would be just to spin ourselves into making everything okay. Just tell ourselves truth over and over and not allow ourselves to feel. The harder thing to do is to sit in the darkness, in the feelings, and wait for the sunrise. It comes. Life does move forward and we have a choice of how moving forward looks to us.

Grieving is also the process in which we adjust to the loss, the finality of where life has taken us. Adjusting happens by acknowledging our life with the loss and how that has changed, and how we have changed. We acknowledge our feelings about the loss both in the present and the future. We externalize those feelings, verbally or written, about what we are experiencing. Externalizing what is happening within us is considered actively grieving. Ironically, while this is active, we are choosing to "sit in the darkness" with the grief. We are not choosing a way to self-medicate or avoid the grief; instead, we are looking for ways to embrace it and include it in our story.

Acknowledging our life with the loss included is key to actively grieving. Maybe a significant person in our life has died, we experienced a divorce, we lost a job, we moved, we weren't selected for something we had our hopes set on getting, a friendship has ended, we are enduring infertility or an adoption failed—whatever it is that has happened, we need to acknowledge that loss in our life. When a significant person passes away, it is more noticeable and therefore typically gets acknowledged socially in our life. Sometimes we are given time off from work for bereavement, and others in our life are sensitive to this loss as well. However, some of the other types of losses we can experience don't receive that same attention. It can be hard to acknowledge the loss in your life when it doesn't seem to matter or is recognized by anyone else. We can begin to question if we should even feel the way we are feeling. In both scenarios a loss has happened, and acknowledgment is necessary. Acknowledgment of the loss means giving ourselves time to sit and think through how life will look now.

Engage

Zoom-In (sit in the dark)

- Describe your loss and your grieving. How do you see it affecting your life: emotionally, socially, physically, and cognitively?
- How has it been acknowledged by others? What support have you received?
- What's the hardest part about grief?
- List your secondary losses.

Zoom-Out

- What's changed? What's different today in my daily life?
- What will the future look like now?
- What losses are we going to experience in the future because of this loss?
- What questions or unknowns about your future does this bring up now?
- What feelings do those answers bring up in us?

Grief is hard work. It's hard because most of us would choose to avoid feeling despair and sadness that might come with reflection. But if we can be brave enough and have the courage to sit in that darkness for a bit, the sun will rise again. Write those feelings and thoughts down. Maybe you prefer to draw—that works as well. Sharing with a trusted friend might be helpful as well. Externalize them and do that more than once. One sign that a child is grieving is that they can ask the same question or say the same statement over and over again. Children don't necessarily care or maybe even realize they are doing this. As adults, we are too aware of that. We don't want to burden the people we love with repeating a thought about our loss or with questions that might come up from it. We think we can just handle this on our own. However, we need to talk and process our grief just like children do, and sometimes that looks like repetitive thoughts and conversations. This loss, whatever it is, is now a part of our story. Acknowledging the loss and looking at where the story can go with the loss included is a choice we can make when we actively grieve.

Grieving looks differently for each person. Giving space and grace for this in our relationships is also important. The people in our life who have experienced the loss will have their own perspectives and experiences that shape the way they will grieve. The people in our life who aren't suffering the loss directly but are journeying through it with us may voice their thoughts about how our grieving needs to look at certain points. Although these people care for us deeply, it is helpful to remember everyone will journey at their own pace and in their own time. Giving ourselves time and space where we need it is a vital part of actively grieving. People may not always understand our needs at those moments. That's okay. We can have the courage to do what we need to do for our journey and offer others grace and space as well. Grieving can be a long road with times of easy travel and times of really rocky travel. Remembering that it is all part of grieving and those seasons of rocky travel that will come can be helpful. Sitting in those moments and letting trusted people into them with us can be very healing.

Grieving can strain relationships, and it can seem easier to shut down all the feelings so that we can just do life. Sometimes we are grieving because of a current relationship. Maybe a loved one is unhealthy, either emotionally or physically, and we need to actively grieve the loss even though they are still with us. We grieve the loss of the previous relationship, while we acknowledge that a new one needs to replace it. We can write a letter to them and choose not to send it, and that releases them in the ways we need. We can say what we need to say in that letter and give ourselves a chance to forgive, be sad, angry or hurt, and sit in the darkness. We can acknowledge what we want the new relationship to look like for us, knowing we can only change ourselves.

Sometimes grieving can lead to being numb. It can get exhausting. There are all sorts of reasons we will grieve in this life; our challenge is to face them and give ourselves the time to sit in it long enough to see the sunrise.

CHAPTER 8

SPIRITUAL IMPACT

March 2008, Amy

*I stood in church and didn't feel anything. I listened to the music and the message and still felt nothing. I went home and when I read my Bible, I felt nothing. **I couldn't feel God.** I was having a hard time even understanding what I was reading. It was like nothing could get in no matter what I tried. I was angry at the way life was turning out and it wasn't what I wanted or where I desired to be at all.*

W e have seen the many ways being numb impacts our life. It impacts how we feel, how we react, how we behave, and how we process the world around us. We have seen the impacts on our relationships, too. We cannot have meaningful relationships until we can fully feel and be free in that. There will always be a trigger or a wall in our relationships if we don't do the work of making sure we are emotionally healthy. It not only affects our relationships with others, but it can also affect our relationship with God.

Life can be so hard, it can knock us down in ways we never even thought possible. Jesus told us in John he wants us not to just survive life here on earth, but to have an abundant life.

"I have come that they might have life, and have it to the full."
JOHN 10:10b

If we operate while only in the middle of that feeling spectrum from Chapter 1 and feel "fine," then we aren't living life to the fullest. Engaging our feelings isn't pleasant at all times. However, if we have enough courage, enough strength, and enough patience, there is a better, more fulfilling life waiting for us if we will do the work. It is possible, no matter where we find ourselves, to have an abundant life. We can enjoy life and have one full of profound joy and gladness again.

Abundant life comes from a deeper relationship with Jesus. This relationship will help us find our freedom. It is also the model and starting point for our other relationships. It's where we learn to be loved well and, in turn, love ourselves and others well. It's also the safest place to go because He understands how life can be hard here on earth. We get to know Jesus more intimately when we fellowship with Him in our suffering.

> *"I want to know Christ—yes, to know the power of his resurrection and participation in his sufferings."*
>
> PHILIPPIANS 3:10

Jesus got it. He suffered and He knew trauma. He was betrayed, abandoned by his Father, misunderstood, physically beaten, rejected, and experienced loss of loved ones. These are just some of the things Jesus endured while He walked this earth. When we find ourselves in our own experiences, we know He also gets the vulnerability that we can feel in it. Sometimes it can be hard to let people into our hurting place because not everyone handles it well. Jesus understands our pain, isn't scared off when we walk through it, and won't ever say the wrong thing to us. He is our safe place and will love us no matter what. He can also be an encouragement to us. Suffering wasn't the end of His story, and it doesn't have to be the end of our story. We can experience the abundant life through our deeper relationship with Jesus, who has been there and overcame all that we will go through.

Suffering wasn't the end of His story, and it doesn't have to be the end of our story.

Abundant life also includes deeper relationships with others.

"They devoted themselves to the apostles' teaching and to fellowship, to the breaking of bread and to prayer. Everyone was filled with awe at the many wonders and signs performed by the apostles. All the believers were together and had everything in common. They sold property and possessions to give to anyone who had need."

Acts 2:42–45

Here in Acts we see that they devoted themselves to fellowship. In our world today, we are taught to be independent to the point where we can fool ourselves into thinking we don't need other people. Abundant life doesn't come in isolation. We were made to be in relationship with others. We need connection, we need to be known, and we need to be loved. Having a deeper relationship with Jesus and having healthy relationships with others leads us to feeling more than "fine" and also helps us discover abundant life.

Engage

Zoom-in/Zoom-out

- How are your relationships? With God? With others? With yourself?
- What does abundant life look like to you?
- Are you experiencing abundant life? On a scale of 1–10, how much are you living in abundant life, with 10 representing always and 1 being never?

- Are your relationships with God, others, or yourself in the "fine" part of the spectrum?
- When was the last time you felt excited to spend time with God? Or the last time you felt overwhelmed by His presence?
- When was the last time you felt compassion for others?

What makes us spiritually numb?

Abundant life through a deeper relationship with Jesus and others can be difficult when we are numb. We talked about the relational impact of being numb in the previous chapter, and some of that overlaps into why we can become spiritually numb. Forgiveness, or rather unforgiveness, can build a strong wall in all of our relationships. It creates a barrier that doesn't allow us to have deep relationships because we are too busy making sure that wall is strong enough so we don't get hurt again. Since being open to God and Jesus starts with a relationship, we are unable to move forward if we are ensuring a strong wall is in place instead of that two-way connection. We also become spiritually numb as we live in the paradigm of fear, pain, and shame instead of faith, hope, and love. We cannot sustain the energy to feel bad all the time and we go numb so we don't have to feel all the bad feelings. We don't know how to cope with or find healing in our fear, our pain, or our shame, so we shut down. However, we can learn to forgive and we can learn to live the new paradigm of faith, hope, and love. We can find freedom and reconnect with Jesus, others, and ourselves.

Unforgiveness

Unforgiveness of others, self, and/or God can overwhelm us, shut our emotions down, and cause us to go numb. A good starting point is to ask ourselves whether unforgiveness is present. Perhaps someone in our life has hurt us deeply. Maybe we are angry, even justifiably, but that anger has led to unforgiveness. It could be that we need to forgive ourselves; we have done something that has led to hurt, pain, or shame, and we need to reconcile it within ourselves or with God. Maybe life has beat us down and we feel anger towards God, and it has become a barrier in our relationship with Him.

Forgiveness won't change our past, but it will free our future. It could be the freedom we experience in the next moment as we read this section. In a typical scenario, there is an offended person and the offender. Imagine physical chains as an offense. Once the offense happens, there are now chains placed on the offended by the offender. Because of that, the offended person is emotionally and spiritually bound to the offender by these chains of unforgiveness. As soon as the chains are on, no matter how much distance is between them, there is only one way to break that bond: forgiveness. Ideally, the offender would recognize the need and ask for forgiveness from the offended. This may never happen. The reality is there are probably only a few times

Remaining in the place of unforgiveness is making ourselves sit in a locked prison cell. We think the other person has the key to free us, but in reality we have the key and have always had it.

where we will be asked for forgiveness in our relationships in the case of an offense. Truthfully, even if this does happen, we still own the power to forgive them or not. It falls to the offended to forgive. Imagine those chains again. The offended takes all the chains off the offender and gives up the right for revenge. Giving up the right for revenge is forgiveness. It is giving up the right to inflict harm on the offender in our thoughts, our words, and in our actions. This doesn't mean we bypass justice if justice is required. This means, by definition, we give up our right to inflict harm and we ask God to deal with it instead. The reason this works is that we are no longer bound to the other person. We have removed the chains that kept us locked in to the pain and we have given them over to God. Once they are removed, we can let God help us face the pain that is left over from those chains.

Remaining in the place of unforgiveness is making ourselves sit in a locked prison cell. We think the other person has the key to free us, but in reality we have the key and have always had it. While we are angry or hurt at the other person thinking if they would just do what we think they should do, it would unlock the doors and we could be free. However, we have the key, the power that can open the doors and let ourselves out whenever we want to be released. Forgiveness is a choice you make. Making that choice and asking God to help us is the best way to gain that freedom.

Forgiveness was modeled by Jesus. He was betrayed by some of his closest friends on earth and to this day is still misunderstood and rejected as Lord. Jesus chooses to forgive those closest to him, those who put him to death, and every person who exists.

"They crucified him [Jesus] there, along with the criminals-one on his right and the other on his left. Jesus said, "Father, forgive them, for they do not know what they are doing."

LUKE 23:33b–34

While He was hanging on the cross and experiencing excruciating pain, He had one concern: for all to be forgiven. I can only hope we have a fraction of this love to forgive like He forgives. In order to prevent being numb, we must choose to love and forgive the way God does, and this will cause the chains to fall off us.

If our choices have caused the pain we are enduring, we can hold ourselves captive in the same way. We can continually keep ourselves locked up in pain or shame through unforgiveness. If we are needing to forgive ourselves, we can insert our name instead as we read through the next few paragraphs. It is important to remember we need to forgive and offer ourselves the same grace we are asking to give others.

How to Forgive:

1. Choose it.

"I can do all this through him who gives me strength."

PHILIPPIANS 4:13

It starts with a choice to let go of the chains and release the right to revenge. Daily, minute by minute, or as often as we feel the need to release the chains and not pick them back up. There may be ongoing reasons to forgive. Maybe someone in our life is extremely unhealthy and they continually hurt us.

That would require a daily or minute-by-minute choice to forgive. We must not let the mountain of unforgiveness continue to grow. If we do, the chain of bondage around us tightens. Instead, we must continually break that bondage and choose freedom. Doing these two things are not easy actions to take.

Our minds can get consumed with thoughts and we can ruminate on them. It's vital to make a choice in those moments to stop those thoughts, take them captive, and replace them with forgiveness. A way to take those thoughts captive is to attach a visual to them so when they come flooding in, the visual will pop up too and help us to choose a different option. As those come up, we then replace them with a new thought and a new visual.

For example, think of a painful time that can consume your thoughts and write down the specific thought or thoughts that come up. As we list those thoughts, we imagine the visual of reconnecting the chains locking us both up again. Now replace the thought and imagine the visual of breaking the chain and being free. The idea is that we train ourselves to actively forgive so that when we think of the hurt, we also think of breaking

We intentionally choose what we ultimately want.

off the chains. We imagine being free instead of being locked up and angry. This isn't saying that the person who is hurting us "deserves a pass." Actually, this doesn't have much to do with them at all. We intentionally choose what we ultimately want.

2. Pray for those who hurt us.

> *"Bless those who curse you, pray for those who mistreat you."*
>
> LUKE 6:28

This prayer isn't asking God to harm them but genuinely praying for them. While "what" they have done to us is hurtful, the "why" is where they need God's healing. Pray for God to meet them there. Whether or not we are able to do this becomes a great temperature reading for our heart. If we have a difficult time praying for the offender, we need to check and make sure we haven't reconnected the chains again.

During Jesus' time, the Romans worshiped "revenge" as one of their gods. And in Jewish law, they believed an eye for an eye, tooth for a tooth, and blood for blood. Revenge is retaliation. We are seeking that the offender suffers for what they have done to us. However, Jesus flipped the script in Matthew. "You have heard that it was said, 'Love your neighbor and hate your enemy.' But I tell you, love your enemies and pray for those who persecute you." Matthew 5:43–44

Jesus knew the only way to be free was to hand over the chains. He even goes to the next step of praying for the offenders in our lives. We can pray for them to know the overwhelming love of Jesus. As we hand over the chains and pray for those who have hurt us, the power of unforgiveness decreases and freedom increases.

3. Check ourselves regularly.

"Bear with each other and forgive one another if any of you has a grievance against someone. Forgive as the Lord forgave you."

Colossians 3:13

Take a regular inventory to see if there is unforgiveness present. We need to check in every so often and ask ourselves if there is a need to forgive anyone. Knowing that at some point in the future we will be hurt again, even if it is in a small way, can help us to make checking in a habit. Once we take the inventory and realize we have been hurt, we can go back through the "How to Forgive" section. Forgiveness will be a continual skill we need to engage in for our freedom and healing.

Another way to check ourselves regularly and to not let the mountain of unforgiveness grow is to approach it with humility. We can remember to live in the reality that not one of us is perfect. We may not have done what the offender has done, but we have probably hurt someone at some point in our life. There are sins with deeper consequences, and that might take more time to forgive. Even in that truth, we can still see how we all hurt each other and recognize any sin as sin. See their sin, see it right next to ours, paid for on the cross. We can picture ourselves nailing Jesus to the cross along with that person doing the same. We are all forgiven from imperfect choices we have made. Remembering this will help us to forgive others and to check our attitudes about ourselves, which leads to right actions. Forgiveness is about finding our own healing, not about justifying whether someone deserves it.

If you wait to forgive for when it feels right, when there's been justice, or when it doesn't bother you as much anymore, you may be waiting a long time, maybe even forever. It never feels right to be living in a prison cell of unforgiveness. Their offense may never be justified, and while time may be able to lessen the pain of the offense, it might always bother us. Forgiveness does not mean what happened was okay. It does not mean that we forget what happened. It is choosing to set ourselves free. We humbly recognize that no one is perfect, and their "why" for what they did is where they need God more than anything. Pray for them in that place. When we work through unforgiveness of others, ourselves, and God, we take a step forward into feeling again. Since unforgiveness can take up so much mind and heart space, forgiveness allows our minds to be able to reflect and be intentional on moving toward the abundant life instead.

Engage

- Who do you need to forgive now? Someone else? Yourself? God?
- How do you feel when you are living with unforgiveness?
- What thoughts and visuals come up when you think of that person or event?
- What thoughts and visuals can you use to replace those?
- How have you forgiven people in the past?
- How do you feel when you forgive?

- What person who has hurt you needs healing right now? How can you pray for them?
- What have you been forgiven for and by whom?

Fear, Pain, Shame versus Faith, Hope, Love

Another way to live spiritually numb is to live in these three cages: fear, pain, and shame. These are seen in Genesis 3 at the beginning of mankind and are still present today. They lead us to being spiritually numb because they can paralyze us, cause us to give up, and lead us to pretend to be someone else in ways we might not even recognize. We can live with one, two, or all three of these cages being present in our lives. Awareness of what we are currently experiencing is going to be how we can exchange the cage or cages we are in for the freedom we can have. If we are living in fear and keeping secrets, we can learn how to be free through faith and trust. If we are living in pain and believing lies, we can learn how to be free through hope and truth. If we are living in shame and covering it up with masks, we can learn how to be free through love and transparency. We do not have to stay locked up in fear, pain, and shame. We can choose freedom and instead live in faith, hope, and love.

Fear

Fear can either be a motivator or a demotivator, a positive or negative influence in our life. As a demotivator it tells us, "I am afraid to face the past, so I will just stay here and pretend I am fine" or "I am afraid that I won't be able to come out of the dark hole I'll fall into if I sit in my feelings, so I will just busy

107

myself and not think about it." We tend to value comfort over change. Even if that comfort isn't actually making us very comfortable. It is what we know so we continue on in it, unable to move to a different place. Fear makes the enemy and opposition more significant than it is in reality. Imagine a miniature army man toy sitting on a table. This army man will represent a fear we have. Now imagine we shine a flashlight on that army man; the shadow of the army man cast on the wall becomes giant and overwhelming. It makes the army man seem even more prominent than life size, but in reality it is merely the shadow that is larger. The shadow becomes the focus and in fear we are paralyzed. We see this massive and looming threat and it debilitates us, making the enemy bigger than it is in reality. In fear, we avoid what we need to face to find our freedom. In fear, we are paralyzed and become spiritually numb.

We tend to value comfort over change. Even if that comfort isn't actually making us very comfortable.

We see fear played out through secret keeping. We may not intentionally keep secrets, but we don't share our fears or what is internally going on with us with our trusted people. We choose to stay paralyzed and isolated. Perhaps we don't think anything would change if we talked about it, or it's been there so long that it's just a part of "who we are." Maybe we have lived with it for so long and to talk about it now feels overwhelming; or we don't want people in our life to think differently of us; or we think we have handled it okay and it's not that big of a deal. However, it never quite goes away entirely. We can think we aren't experiencing symptoms from it and that is the danger of avoidance. We don't fully know what is contributing to our reactions, thoughts, or decision-making. We assume that those secrets, whether intentional or unintentional, aren't a part of it. But I have seen in counseling where it is almost always the lie that accompanies secrets. We make choices to avoid the facing of our fear, and we react and base our thoughts on our fear because that shadow is our focus. The secret keeping and keeping trusted people at a distance by not letting them know our fear is the symptom of living in the cage of fear.

Pain

Pain can be defined by mental, emotional, or physical suffering or discomfort in our lives. Pain could be something from our past, something we are experiencing now, or even an emotional distress that comes with hopelessness in not seeing a future that would be pain-free. In Genesis 3, we see God tell Adam and Eve that life is not going to come easy anymore. This cursed world won't be fair and is going to bite us back. It can hurt, and it can be painful.

Take the example of the grown elephant held outside a circus tent by a small stake in the ground. That grown elephant could easily rip the wooden stake out of the ground, but it doesn't because the elephant believes a lie. When elephant trainers train baby elephants, they will use heavy chains and a sturdy iron anchor bar that they drive deep into the ground. When the baby elephant tugs and tries to get away, he can't and experiences the pain of the shackle on his leg. Eventually, the baby elephant gives up and stops pulling. As the elephant grows up, the trainer replaces the iron anchor bar with a wooden stake and sometimes the chain with a rope. So an animal that can weigh up to 7 tons is tied down, limited to a particular area, not able to run wild like he was designed for, all because of a 2 x 4 piece of wood and rope. The problem is not the stake in the ground keeping him in place; it's the pain from his past that keeps him there. He believes he can't move from it, so he doesn't. In our lives, too, we think we aren't ever going to get past the pain, so we don't even try—we give up. To sustain the giving-up posture, we become spiritually numb.

Maybe like the elephant, we have got much more power and strength than we can fathom, yet we are convinced of the lie that what's tied us down in our past has our present and our future tied down as well. What kind of self-talk is present? If we had a script of the things we tell ourselves, what lies would we be able to recognize? The most common lies are the ones we tell ourselves. "I'm not good enough," "It will never get better," "I'm not worth it," "No one cares" are a few examples. We tell ourselves lies because somewhere in us we think that is easier to accept than the pain we are experiencing. Or we choose to inflict more pain by the lies of unworthiness and hopelessness. Believing and saying these lies to ourselves as if they are truth is a symptom of living in a cage of pain.

Shame

Shame is defined as a feeling of guilt, regret, disgrace, or sadness that we have because we know we have done something wrong or something wrong has been done to us. In the Bible, Adam and Eve were ashamed and hid. Symptoms of shame include hiding or trying to cover up that wrong action, embarrassment from thoughts we might be having, or of someone finding out about the wrong that was done by us or to us. Shame leads us to pretend that we are "fine" and not letting people see the truth. To sustain the constant hiding and pretending, we become spiritually numb.

We put on a face to show people that everything is "great" and that we are "feeling fine." When, in reality, on the inside we are numb and experiencing very much the opposite. We become good at performing by keeping on the masks. We don't even remember just how long it has been since we have allowed ourselves to feel and not pretend. At times, we may even start to believe that the masks are who we are now. Maybe we aren't intentionally putting on a mask to be fake, but we are still doing it as perceived protection for ourselves or others. We don't let people into the shame we are feeling. Masking where or who we are is a symptom of living in a cage of shame.

Freedom

> *"And now these three remain: faith, hope, and love. But the greatest of these is love."*
>
> 1 CORINTHIANS 13:13

From Genesis 3 to now, thousands of years later, these cages of fear, pain, and shame are still at play in directing us. These have become the filters in how many of our choices are made or influenced. They have paralyzed us, they have caused us to give up, and they have led us to pretend. We stay locked in these cages by keeping secrets, believing lies, and wearing masks. These symptoms all occur in darkness and in isolation from others. To combat those cages, we need a new paradigm from which to live. We bring everything out into the light. We leave behind the isolation and we let others into our darkness. When it is in the light, we can see what needs to change and then deal with it. We bring fear and secrets, pain and lies, shame and masks out onto the table. We sort through it and figure out what needs to get replaced, and we allow God and others into it too. From there we can learn to live in faith, hope, and love. We replace fear and secrets with faith and trust; pain and lies with hope and truth, shame and masks with love and transparency. Through this new paradigm, we find our freedom and healing from being numb.

Fear to Faith

"And we know that in all things God works for the good of those who love him, who have been called according to his purpose."

ROMANS 8:28

Where fear once paralyzed us, we see faith that tells us we aren't alone. We can trust God to help us process all the possible feelings of deep sadness so that we can move past feeling "fine" and feel deep joy again. We can know that no matter what happens, no matter how big those shadows of army men look, we trust it will be okay when we face them. We trust through faith that when we go to the dark places, we have One who is working before us in all things and for our ultimate good. Shifting our focus from the shadow to the actual fear also helps us know what exactly is making us paralyzed. We can name the fear and how it's keep-ing us from moving. Don't keep it a secret anymore. Sometimes just taking that step diminishes some of the fear that feels so big. We may need to face the fear more than once. Each time we address the fear, it loses some of

> *Each time we address the fear, it loses some of its grip and power on us.*

its grip and power on us. Bringing someone else into that fear with us and talking about it can help not only take the fear out of the darkness and isolation, but we can also gain a different perspective. When we replace our secrets with trust of God and others, we gain freedom. Fear doesn't have to paralyze us. In faith, we can trust that God has got us and we have more power than whatever it is that has held us.

Pain to Hope

"God did this so that, by two uchangeable things in which it is impossible for God to lie, we who have fled to take hold of the hope set before us may be greatly encouraged. We have this hope as an anchor for the soul, firm and secure."

HEBREWS 6:18–19a

Where pain once caused us to give up, we can have a hope that endures. We can realize our strength. We use truth to stop us from believing the lies that have held us captive in one place. Making sure to tell ourselves truth instead of lies is an important part of changing the paradigm and not living spiritually numb. If we believe we are not worth it, if we believe that nothing will change, and if we believe that we are not strong enough or good enough, then we will never move from that place, just like the elephant. Truth is all it would take for the elephant to unbind itself from a simple rope and stake. Believing, remembering, and knowing the truth would give the elephant freedom. Believing that we are worthy because God says we are His child, knowing that we don't have to stay in the pain we are in, and remembering we have power because God has given us His strength bring that freedom. Whatever the lie that has been circulating in our life, replace it with the truth. Truth can move us through our pain. It doesn't always take it away, but it moves us to hope. Hope helps us see the bigger picture and a future again. Hope is a strong and trustworthy anchor for our souls.

Shame to Love

"From him the whole body, joined and held together by every supporting ligament, grows and builds itself up in love, as each part does its work."

EPHESIANS 4:16

Where shame once had us wearing masks, we can now have the love that is perfect and unconditional. We don't have to pretend anymore because we know that no matter what, God loves us and He already knows all of our stories. Through love, we can take off the masks we wear and begin to live in transparency with God and others. Transparency can feel scary, but freedom comes when we take off the masks and let go of our shame. Once we stop pretending to be someone or something else and let others into our stories, we can find freedom.

Connection with people is vital. We might live in a place where transparency is not the norm for our culture, and it can be difficult to figure out how to begin connecting with others and growing with them. Transparency can be gradual as the relationship grows and deepens. Find a trusted person, seek connection, and begin to share your stories. Transparency can lead to knowing a love that is perfect and from this perfect love, we can love others well.

We see that there is overlap in the three cages. Masks are a type of secret and lie; a secret can lead us to wearing a mask and telling a lie; and a lie can lead us to wearing a mask and keeping a secret. One experience can lead to us being locked in all three cages. It is important to identify and call out the source from where our thoughts and behaviors originate. The new paradigm of faith, hope, and love offers us freedom to live the abundant life. We now have tools and ways to combat the old way of thinking and living. No longer do we need to depend on secrets, lies, and masks to get us through surviving life. Instead, we can use trust, truth, and transparency to heal and move us forward.

August 2000, Jake

While I was filling out a form, a question was asked about my past and whether or not I have been abused. I struggled with what to

115

*write down. **I lied.** I marked down that I haven't been molested even though I was when I was little. I don't remember exactly how old I was when it happened, and my parents don't even know it happened. I haven't talked about it to anyone ever before. Why should I talk about it? It's in the past, it's not who I am. Plus, **I am not sure what people would really think of me.** I don't want them seeing that when they look at me. I don't want to be known for what happened to me.*

In this story, we see all three cages at play. We see fear and secrets. He is afraid of what people will think of him, or if he will even be able to serve as a counselor, so he lied on the application. Now that is a new secret for him to keep. We see pain and lies. He is stuck, tied to his past, and believing the lie that he isn't good enough. We see shame and masks the most here. He put on a front different from the truth and is ashamed of what happened to him. He won't let others into his story, not even his parents. He keeps what happened to him isolated from others and in the darkness, and he is constantly pretending that everything was fine. These actions end up trapping him in ways he can't fully see until he shifts his paradigm.

What if he replaced the secret with trust? He could then let trusted people into his story and end up telling the truth on his application. That would exchange the lies for the truth of not being good enough because none of this was his fault. He doesn't need to carry or own someone else's painful choice. He is good enough because he is a child of God. He took off his mask and shared the story with his parents, and now also shares it with anyone whom he thinks it will help. He has found freedom by identifying what was keeping him locked up and choosing to live in another paradigm. This story doesn't paralyze him anymore. Instead, it has become a way for others to find freedom too.

Engage

Zoom-in

- Name the fear that is keeping you paralyzed. What is your looming shadow of fear?
- How can you face the fear? What does that look like for you?
- What secrets have you kept?
- With what trusted person, in addition to God, can you share this fear and/or secrets?

Zoom-out

- What fears have you conquered or been open about before? What happened to those fears?
- How does your faith free you from fear?

Zoom-in

- What pain has you stuck in the past or has caused you to give up?
- What lies have you believed?
- What truth will replace those lies?

Zoom-out

- What pain or lies have you experienced in the past that now truth has replaced?
- How does hope free you from your pain?

Zoom-in

- What shame are you carrying with you? In what ways are you pretending?
- What masks are present in your life? When have you told a trusted person that you were "fine" instead of letting them into your shame?
- In what ways can you be transparent with God and others? What are the differences and similarities between transparency and honesty?
- With what trusted person can you share your story?

Zoom-out

- What masks or shame have you let go of in the past? What was that like for you? How has that become a part of your story to help others?
- How does love free you from your shame?

CHAPTER 9

GROWING IN FEELINGS

January 2017, Josh

*I was at work driving to a job when I got an email. I noticed I was pretty upset after reading this email. Before getting out of the car to jump into work, I sat in my car for a minute and started to cry. I called a trusted friend to talk through what just happened. My dad is in the hospital and probably won't live much longer, and I knew that was also upsetting me. **As I externalized and processed more, I discovered** the email triggered a realization that I don't have the needed support and connection I really desire for when my dad does pass away. I am grieving.*

Doing the work of processing our feelings isn't always easy or fun, but when we begin to do it more regularly, we start to see the benefits. Much like working out, it becomes easier and we get stronger from it. It becomes more natural to sit in feelings and ask the questions that lead us to a place where we can make choices about what we want to do. We are more in control. We feel more than just the middle of the road: we can feel deep joy finally. We feel free from merely surviving the everyday life and we have insight about ourselves and the relationships in our life. Much like my friend in the story above, years of being intentional and sitting with his feelings allowed him to quickly realize, in this instant, there was more going on than the circumstance right in front of his face. The email was able to trigger an overreaction and he instantly knew there was more to discover. That entire process maybe took him 15 minutes. The reality is he has a lot going on but he didn't go numb because of it. Instead, he gained some insights and perspectives that guided him intentionally, not reactively. As we take time to build on each of the blocks we have now given ourselves in this book, the process will become more fluid and natural.

As we grow in our skills, we learn which of our feelings need specific attention.

We know how to identify if we are numb. We know whether we are stuck in the box of feeling "fine" or if we are feeling deeper joy or sadness. We gain perspective on how we became numb, either by a flood of feelings we are unable to process at once or by shutting down over time. We recognize the different symptoms of being numb and why we can't ultimately sustain any of those for a long amount of time. As we practice the zoom-out skill, these blocks allow for us to see what we have overcome and perceive when it seems to be happening again. Life doesn't slow down, and will continue to throw us curveballs we must learn to handle. As we grow in our skills, we learn which of our feelings need specific attention. The feelings that seem stronger or that elicit a reaction can be prompts for this process of intentionality. We can take those through the Feelings Guide and give ourselves some time to assess them. Remaining in the balanced perspective of zoom-in and zoom-out is how we grow in our feelings.

Even though we have been intentional and have offered time to ourselves, we may find once again that we are numb. We can go back and check in on each of the building blocks we have gained and see which ones need some application this time around. We can answer the Notes questions and gain new insights and perspectives that will add to our strong and growing zoom-out tree.

In the same way, there is no perfect avenue to get back to feeling, for we all grow in feeling in different ways. The idea is that we get stronger, and using the tools gets easier as we move along. We are stronger than we think we are. We may see people in our life and think, *I don't know how they made it through_____, I could never survive that*. The truth is others may look at us and think that they could have never survived what we have been through. We all have our journey, and we are stronger than we think we are.

- We have decided to do more than survive.
- We have chosen to love ourselves and others well.
- We have chosen to put a purpose to things that have happened to us, in us, or through us. We chose to face the feelings and not avoid the pain.
- We made a courageous choice to actively grieve and sit in the darkness for a little bit and wait for the sun to rise.
- We made a decision to have an abundant life, to not only feel some deep sadness but also feel deep joy and move from the middle of the spectrum.

Because of this choice we are stronger now, and we have a strong foundation. We are not easily shaken.

A big part of the balanced perspective and one that gets overlooked so often is celebrating. Feeling again is a gift that we have given ourselves, and we can celebrate that we aren't where we once were: we have grown. Oftentimes in therapy, my job includes reminding the client that they aren't where they were a week, a month, or a year ago. As humans, we just want to feel good, to experience joy, and to move on from the pain in which we find ourselves. Yet we think that equals *never* experiencing bad and *never* experiencing sadness and pain. Instead, we need to celebrate the times that we have that are truly good, joyful, exciting, and fulfilling. We get so blinded by the negative it

> Feeling again is a gift that we have given ourselves, and we can celebrate that we aren't where we once were: we have grown.

122

becomes all we see. I will ask my clients to quantify, if possible, how much of their week was good and how much was painful. We zoom in to the painful and talk about that while being balanced as we zoom out and celebrate the good. Sometimes the good is simply not settling for feeling "fine" and facing the pain. Not just merely surviving is a huge accomplishment and life-giving for ourselves. We celebrate together and in that we find thankfulness.

When we learn to celebrate and find those accomplishments, we give ourselves and others freedom and healing. Relationships are a vital building block of this book. We see how relationships can offer us a mirror into ourselves, they can help us find freedom, through them we can break negative cycles and create positive cycles, and help heal our communities as we become healthier. I am personally encouraged to be in this community as we all continue to grow stronger, to feel again, and to love well!

Engage

List some examples that you can celebrate.

- The good relationships that love and encourage you
- The good things happening in and around you
- The gifts you have
- The change and choices that you can make in your own life
- Being able to feel